Mystical
Poems of
Rūmī

UNESCO COLLECTION
OF REPRESENTATIVE WORKS

THIS VOLUME HAS BEEN ACCEPTED IN THE
TRANSLATIONS SERIES OF PERSIAN WORKS
JOINTLY SPONSORED BY
THE ROYAL INSTITUTE OF TRANSLATION OF TEHERAN,
AND THE UNITED NATIONS EDUCATIONAL,
SCIENTIFIC AND CULTURAL ORGANIZATION (UNESCO)

Mystical Poems of Rūmī

Translated from the Persian
By A. J. Arberry

THE UNIVERSITY OF CHICAGO PRESS
Chicago and London

The University of Chicago Press, Chicago 60637
The University of Chicago Press, Ltd., London
Published 1968
Printed in the United States of America
Library of Congress Catalog Card Number: 68–29935
86 85 84   8765

Contents

Introduction

Jalāl al-Dīn Rūmī, author of a vast collection of Persian odes and lyrics, of which a selection is here offered in translation, was born in A.D. 1207 at Balkh, which now lies within the frontiers of Afghanistan, and died in 1273 at Konya, in Asiatic Turkey. For an account of his life and times, the reader is invited to peruse the preface to my version of Rūmī's *Fīhi mā fīhi*, published by John Murray in 1961 under the title *Discourses of Rumi;* there is nothing I wish to add to what is written there, except by way of stressing the curious circumstances which attended Rūmī's transformation from sober theologian and preacher into ecstatic dancer and enraptured poet.

Rūmī's father, Bahā' al-Dīn Valad, had attained eminence in religious circles in Khorasan before his headlong flight to Saljūq Turkey on the eve of the Mongol invasions; in Konya, where he died in 1230, he enjoyed royal patronage and popular esteem as preacher and teacher. From 1240 to 1244, having completed his long formal education in Aleppo and Damascus, Rūmī in his own turn taught and preached in Konya. Then, in 1244, when Rūmī was already thirty-seven years of age and seemingly set in his ways as a conventional mullah, a wandering dervish named Shams al-Dīn, a native of Tabriz apparently of artisan origin, suddenly arrived in the Saljūq capital and attracted attention by the wildness of his demeanour.

"Jalāl al-Dīn," wrote R. A. Nicholson in his *Rumi, Poet and Mystic,*[1] "found in the stranger that perfect image of the Divine Beloved which he had long been seeking. He took him away to his house, and for a year or two they remained inseparable. Sultān Valad (Rūmī's son and biographer) likens his father's all-absorbing communion with this 'hidden saint' to the celebrated journey of Moses in company with Khaḍir (Koran, XVIII 64–80), the sage whom Sufis regard as the supreme hierophant and guide of travellers on the Way to God. Rūmī's pupils resented their teacher's preoccupation with the eccentric stranger, and vilified and intrigued against him until Shams al-Dīn fled to Damascus. Rūmī sent his son to bring him back; but the tongues of his jealous traducers soon wagged again, and presently, perhaps in

---

[1] P. 19.

1

1247, the man of mystery vanished without leaving a trace behind."

The intense excitement of these adventures transformed Jalāl al-Dīn from the sober divine into an ecstatic wholly incapable of controlling the torrent of poetry which now poured forth from him. To symbolize, it is said, the search for the lost Beloved, now identified with Shams al-Dīn, he invented the famous whirling and circling dance of his Mevlevi dervishes, performed to the accompaniment of the lamenting reed pipe and the pacing drum. Night was turned into day in the long mystical orgy, and from time to time under the impact of the passionate moment Jalāl al-Dīn uttered extempore brief quatrains or extended lyrics, which his disciples hastily transcribed and committed to memory. To confess the human source of his inspiration, he very often introduced into his lyrics the name of Shams al-Dīn; later he similarly commemorated Shams al-Dīn's successor in his spiritual affection, Salāh al-Dīn Zarkūb. At other times Rūmī signed his verses with the soubriquet Khāmūsh, the Silent, a reference to the ineffable nature of the mysteries.

Though no manuscript copy of these poems has survived which had been compiled during Rūmī's lifetime, it is certain (as the learned editor Professor Badī' al-Zamān Furūzānfar has pointed out) that such a collection was made, and was available to the scribe of one of the existing codices, dated 723/1323. Nor is this all; it is equally certain that the copyist of another, undated but very ancient, codex had access to material in the autograph of Rūmī himself. Fortunately, several manuscripts have been preserved dating from within fifty years or so from the poet's death, and these have all been collated to serve as a very solid basis for Professor Furūzānfar's edition.[2] The total output, excluding stanza-poems, quatrains and other minor pieces, amounts to 3229 separate odes, in 34,662 couplets. In the course of making the present versions, I have collated once more with the printed text the magnificent Chester Beatty codex, used by the editor in a microfilm which I caused to be made for him; I have noted numerous places where the readings of this codex, sometimes superior to the printed text, have been overlooked by the editor.

The Chester Beatty codex, besides being close to the poet's lifetime and on the whole very correct, exhibits a unique feature to

[2] *Kullīyāt-i Shams.*

which attention may be once more drawn. The Persian ode (Qasīda), like its shorter derivative the lyric (Ghazal), was composed in monorhyme, each couplet terminating in the same vowel+consonant as that chosen to end the opening line. The poet was free to choose between some dozen or so metres, but having made his choice he was required to keep strictly to it throughout the length of the individual composition. Medieval editors and copyists, when they came to publish the collected works (dīvān) of a poet, arranged the pieces not chronologically, nor according to style or subject, but alphabetically according to rhyme, ignoring differences of metre. Now in the Chester Beatty manuscript of Rūmī's Dīvān, the poems have been arranged group by group according to metre; then, within each group, alphabetically by rhyme. Moreover, the opening couplet of each separate poem has been inscribed in red ink, to facilitate speedy identification. The resulting impression is of a gigantic hymn-book; and this indeed may well have been the intention. When it is remembered that these poems were originally composed, and were thereafter chanted, as accompaniment to the sacred dance of the Mevlevi dervishes, it does not seem too fantastic to conclude that the Chester Beatty codex, which once belonged to a Mevlevi monastery in Cairo, was compiled after this fashion as a service book, to help the cantor to choose speedily the poem appropriate in rhythm to the particular phase of the dance.

Rūmī was by no means the first Persian to compose mystical poetry.[3] He had not a few predecessors (and they had predecessors who wrote in Arabic) who gradually established conventions of language, imagery and rhetoric. The most eminent and influential of these pioneers were Sanā'ī, who died circa A.D. 1150, and Farīd al-Dīn 'Attār, whom Rūmī met in his youth.

> Attar was the spirit,
> Sana'i his eyes twain,
> And in time thereafter
> Came we in their train.

So Rūmī acknowledged his debt to these great masters, each of whom left behind a large quantity of mystical odes, as well as

[3] For a brief account of the history of Persian mystical poetry prior to Rūmī, see my Muslim Saints and Mystics (the first volume in the Persian Heritage Series, Chicago and London, 1966), pp. 5–11. It is hoped to go into more detail in the introduction to a second volume of translations of Rūmī's poems, now being prepared.

didactic, epic verse. But he did not confine his reading and admiration to the mystical poets. We know, for instance, that he particularly appreciated the work of the great Arab heroic poet al-Mutanabbī (d. A.D. 955), from whom he quotes in his *Discourses,* as also occasionally in his *Dīvān.* His many nature-poems, especially those on the glories of spring, recall many models amongst the secular Arab and Persian poets. From these and other clues we are able to build up a picture of a man deeply immersed in the poetic traditions of Islam. Yet poetry was very far from being the centre of Rūmī's life; before everything he was a learned theologian after the finest pattern of medieval Islam, very familiar with the Koran and its exegesis, the traditional sayings of the Prophet Muhammad, the sacred law and its erudite expositors, the wranglings of the "Two-and-Seventy jarring sects," not to mention the "foreign sciences" including philosophy, and the lives and dicta of the saints and mystics. All this various learning is reflected in Rūmī's poetry; and it is this fact, coupled with abstruseness of thought and exotic convention of expression, that stands in the way of easy understanding and ready appreciation.

Whereas the interpreter of the *Mathnavī,* Rūmī's massive epic poem on the mystical life, can have recourse to a number of medieval commentaries to assist him in his task, no such aid is available to the student of the *Dīvān.* On the other hand we are very fortunate in possessing R. A. Nicholson's magnificent eight-volume edition, translation, and commentary of the *Mathnavī,* as well as his remarkable primitias, the *Selected Poems from the Dīvāni Shamsi Tabrīz,* with its astonishingly mature and luminous introduction, together with his many other writings on Islamic mysticism, and the precious memory of his personal teaching. (The *Selected Poems* contains only forty-eight pieces, and even so includes a number of poems not found in the oldest manuscripts, and therefore of very doubtful authenticity.) We can also draw upon the erudite writings of Professor Furūzānfar, who has dedicated a lifetime of arduous and unremitting labour to the study of Rūmī. From the medieval period we can rely, albeit cautiously, on the *Manāqib al-'ārifīn* of Shams al-Dīn Aflākī, completed in 1353, a hagiography of Rūmī and his circle which purports to give the circumstances under which a number of the poems were composed. We are also grateful to have Rūmī's "table-talk" in the *Fīhi mā fīhi,* probably compiled by his son Sultān Valad, in the excellent edition of Professor Furūzānfar.

Finally, I have had the good fortune to read all the poems chosen for translation with my learned friend and colleague Dr. Ḥasan Javādī-Tabrīzī, who has made numerous corrections and suggestions for the improvement of this interpretation. These versions, being in the vast majority the first renderings into a western language (and the modern Turkish translation has been fully consulted), and intended primarily for non-specialists, have been made as literal as possible, with a minimal concession to readability. Short notes have been appended, to clarify obscurities and to explain unfamiliar allusions. For the rest, the reader is earnestly advised to make himself familiar with the *Mathnavī* in Nicholson's translation, and with the *Fīhi mā fīhi* in my own *Discourses of Rūmī*. The poet is always consistent in his thought, and often repetitive in his expression, so that all his writings shed an abundance of mutually clarifying light. When all is said and done, however, it must be admitted that a number of passages in these poems still baffle the understanding, which is hardly surprising, considering the occasional nature of some of the references (for these poems were the spontaneous utterances of an ecstatic, unpremeditated and unrevised). There is also the further difficulty, that the language of the poems, though of course greatly influenced by literary style, is basically colloquial. It incorporates many Khorasanian idioms, affected by long residence in Arabic-speaking and Turkish-speaking lands, all from seven hundred years ago, so that the colloquial usages of the present day are not always a reliable guide. Rūmī himself appears to have been conscious of the elusive, evanescent nature of his utterances, as when he says (in poem 125 of this selection), "My verse resembles the bread of Egypt—night passes over it, and you cannot eat it any more."

Rūmī affected an astonishing contempt for his own poetry. On one occasion he remarked, "I am affectionate to such a degree that when these friends come to me, for fear that they may be wearied I speak poetry so that they may be occupied with that. Otherwise, what have I to do with poetry? By Allah, I care nothing for poetry, and there is nothing worse in my eyes than that. It has become incumbent upon me, as when a man plunges his hands into tripe and washes it out for the sake of a guest's appetite, because the guest's appetite is for tripe." The poet's modesty, rooted in a puritanical scrupulosity, does not need to affect our judgment. In Rūmī we encounter one of the world's greatest poets. In profundity of thought, inventiveness of image, and triumphant mastery of language, he stands out as the supreme genius of Islamic mysticism. He invites and deserves the most attentive and intensive study, by a succession of devoted scholars, whose combined explorations will vastly improve upon our first halting attempt. Future generations, as his poetry becomes wider known and more perfectly understood, will enjoy and applaud with increasing insight and enthusiasm the poems of this wisest, most penetrating, and saintliest of men.

The poems that follow are not a continuous cycle, but a careful selection from the first 1,500 odes and lyrics. They thus represent a planned selection, my purpose being to include poems of various styles and degrees of difficulty. The numbering 1–200 is my own, but in the notes I have in every case given the reference to the corresponding number in the Tehran edition.

I

What excuses have you to offer, my heart, for so many short-comings? Such constancy on the part of the Beloved, such unfaithfulness on your own!

So much generosity on his side, on yours such niggling contrariness! So many graces from him, so many faults committed by you!

Such envy, such evil imaginings and dark thoughts in your heart, such drawing, such tasting, such munificence by him!

Why all this tasting? That your bitter soul may become sweet. Why all this drawing? That you may join the company of the saints.

5   You are repentant of your sins, you have the name of God on your lips; in that moment he draws you on, so that he may deliver you alive.

You are fearful at last of your wrongdoings, you seek desperately a way to salvation; in that instant why do you not see by your side him who is putting such fear into your heart?

If he has bound up your eyes, you are like a pebble in his hand; now he rolls you along like this, now he tosses you in the air.

Now he implants in your nature a passion for silver and gold and women; now he implants in your soul the light of the form of Muṣṭafā.

On this side drawing you towards the lovely ones, on that side drawing you to the unlovely; amid these whirlpools the ship can only pass through or founder.

10   Offer up so many prayers, weep so sorely in the night season, that the echo may reach your ears from the sphere of the seven heavens.

When Shu'aib's groaning and lamentation and tears like hailstones passed beyond all bounds, in the morning a proclamation came to him from heaven:

"If you are a sinner, I have forgiven you and granted you pardon for your sins. Is it paradise you seek? Lo, I have given it to you; be silent, cease these petitions!"

Shu'aib retorted, "I seek neither this nor that. What I desire is to see God face to face; though the seven seas all turn to fire, I will plunge therein if only I may encounter Him.

7

But if I am banished from that spectacle, if my tear-stained eyes are shut against that vision, I am more fit to dwell in hellfire; paradise becomes me not.

15 Without His countenance, paradise for me is hateful hell. I am consumed by this hue and scent of mortality; where is the splendour of the lights of immortality?"

They said, "At least moderate your weeping, lest your sight be diminished, for the eye becomes blind when weeping passes beyond bounds."

He said, "If my two eyes in the end should be seeing after that fashion, every part of me will become an eye: why then should I grieve over blindness?

But if in the end this eye of mine should be deprived forever, let that sight indeed become blind which is unworthy to behold the Beloved!"

In this world, every man would become a ransom for his beloved; one man's beloved is a bag of blood, another's the sun in splendour.

20 Since every man has chosen a beloved, good or bad, as suits his own nature, it would be a pity if we should annihilate ourselves for the sake of nothing!

One day a traveller was accompanying Bā Yazīd on a certain road. Presently Bā Yazīd said to him, "What trade have you chosen, you rogue?"

The man replied, "I am an ass-driver." Bā Yazīd exclaimed, "Be gone from me!—Lord, grant that his ass may die, that he may become the slave of God!"

2

O lovers, lovers, this day you and we are fallen into a whirlpool: who knows how to swim?

Though the world's torrent should overflow and every wave become like a dromedary, why shall the waterfowl worry? It is the bird of the air that should be anxious.

Our faces are lighted up with gratitude, schooled as we are in wave and sea, inasmuch as ocean and flood are life-increasing to the fish.

Elder, hand us a towel; water, let us plunge into you; Moses son of 'Imrān, come, smite the water of the sea with your staff!

5   This wind concocts in every head a different passion; let my passion be for yonder cupbearer, and you may have all the rest!

Yesterday yon saki on the way snatched the caps of the drunkards; today he is giving yet more wine, preparing to strip us of our robes.

O envy of the Moon and of Jupiter, with us, yet hidden from sight like a peri, gently, gently you are drawing me on—will you not say whither?

Wherever you go, you are with me still, you who are my eyes and my brightness; if you will, draw me to drunkenness, if you will, transport me to annihilation.

Know that the world is like Mount Sinai, and we like Moses are seekers; every moment an epiphany arrives and cleaves the mountain asunder.

10 One portion becomes green, one portion becomes narcissus-white; one portion becomes a pearl, one portion ruby and amber.

You who seek to behold Him, gaze upon this mountainchain of His. O mountain, what wind has blown upon you? We have become intoxicated with the echo.

O gardener, gardener, why have you come to grapple with us? If we have carried off your grapes, you have carried off our purse!

3

Today I beheld the beloved, that ornament of every affair; he went off departing to heaven like the spirit of Muṣṭafā.

The sun is put to shame by his countenance, heaven's sphere is as confused as the heart; through his glow, water and clay are more resplendent than fire.

"I said, "Show me the ladder, that I may mount up to heaven." He said, "Your head is the ladder; bring your head down under your feet."

When you place your feet on your head, you will place your feet on the head of the stars; when you cleave through the air, set your foot on the air, so, and come!

5   A hundred ways to heaven's air become manifest to you; you
go flying up to heaven every dawning like a prayer.

4

Every instant a revelation from heaven comes to men's inner-
most souls: "How long like dregs do you remain upon earth?
Come up!"

Whoever is heavy of soul in the end proves to be dregs; only
then does he mount to the top of the vat when his dregs are
clarified.

Do not stir the clay every moment, so that your water may
become clear, so that your dregs may be illumined, so that your
pains may be cured.

It is spiritual, like a torch, only its smoke is greater than its
light; when its smoke passes beyond bounds, it no longer displays
radiance in the house.

5   If you diminish the smoke, you will enjoy the light of the
torch; both this abode and that will become illumined by your
light.

If you look into muddy water, you see neither the moon nor
the sky; sun and moon both disappear when darkness possesses
the air.

A northern breeze is blowing, through which the air becomes
clarified; it is for the sake of this burnishing that at dawn the
zephyr breathes.

The spiritual breeze burnishes the breast of all sorrow; let the
breath be stopped but for a moment, and annihilation will come
upon the spirit.

The soul, a stranger in the world, is yearning for the city of
placelessness; why, O why does the bestial spirit continue so long
to graze?

10   Pure, goodly soul, how long will you journey on? You are the
King's falcon; fly back toward the Emperor's whistle!

5

O lovers, lovers, the time of union and encounter has come. The proclamation from heaven has come: "Moon-faced beauties, welcome hither!"

Joyous hearts, joyous hearts, joy has come skirt a-trailing; we have seized its chain, it has seized our skirts.

The fiery potion has come; demon sorrow, sit in a corner; death-anxious soul, depart; immortal saki, enter in!

The seven spheres of heaven are drunk with passion for you; we are as counters in your hand; our being through your being is a myriad times at ease.

5   Sweet-breathed minstrel, every instant shake the bell; O gladness, saddle your steed; O zephyr, blow upon our souls!

O sound of the sweet-conversing reed, in your note is the taste of sugar; your note brings me night and morning the scent of fidelity.

Make beginning again, play those airs once more; O sun lovely of presence, glory over all the lovely ones!

Be silent, do not rend the veil; drain the flagon of the silent ones; be a veiler, be a veiler, habituate yourself to the clemency of God.

6

How sweet it is to give speech and head, to converse with his lip, especially when he opens the door and says, "Good sir, come in!"

To the dry lip he tells the story of the fountain of Khiḍar; according to the stature of the man the tailor of his love cuts the gown.

The fountains become drunken through the intoxication of his eye; the trees are dancing before the gentle breeze of dawn.

The nightingale says to the rosebush, "What is in your heart? Declare it this instant. No other is near; only you and I."

5   The rosebush answers, "So long as you are with yourself,

entertain not this ambition. Make a special effort to transport the burden of your selfhood out of this earthly abode."

The eye of the needle of passion is narrow; know for a certainty that it will not admit any thread when it perceives it to be of double strand.

Behold how the sun is up to the throat in fire, so that through its face the face of the earth may become full of light.

When Moses proceeded towards the burning bush, the bush said, "I am the water of Kauthar; take off your shoes, and come!

Do not fear my fire, for I am water and sweet at that; you have come to prosperity; the seat of honour is yours, welcome!

10   You are a pearl of pure lustre, a ruby of the mine, the soul of place and placelessness; you are the nonpareil of the age; where are other creatures beside you?"

Through love's hand, every hand becomes the royal court of munificence; through you, the faithless world becomes the factory of fidelity.

At the first hour of day you came, in your hand the royal bowl; you are drawing my soul towards the feast, saying, "Welcome!"

What becomes of the heart, when the heart's hand grasps the hand of a sweetheart? What becomes of the dross copper, when it hears the welcoming voice of the philosopher's stone?

A wondrous darling came, in his hand a lance, like a bedouin. I said, "What service can I render?" He said, "Come up to me!"

15   My heart leaped, saying, "Shall I run?" My reason said, "Shall I go?" Generously he signaled, saying, "Yes, both of you!"

Since the table has come down from heaven, wash your hands and your mouth too, that there may not proceed from your palms the odour of onions and chives.

The mine of salt has arrived; take heed, if you are goodly and a lover. Seize the bowl, and give the cup; choose riot, not broth!

Now I close these two lips, so that the lamp of day and night even with the flame of the tongue may tell you the whole story.

7

The king has come, the king has come; adorn the palace-hall; cut your forearms in honour of the fair one of Canaan.

Since the Soul of the soul of the soul has come, it is not meet
to mention the soul; in his presence of what use is the soul, save
as a sacrifice?

Without love I was one who had lost the way; of a sudden
love entered. I was a mountain; I became a straw for the horse of
the king.

Whether he be Turk or Tajik, this slave is near to him even as
soul to body; only the body does not behold the soul.

5 Ho, my friends, good luck has arrived; the time has come for
offering up the load; a Solomon has come to the throne, to
depose Satan.

Leap from your place; why do you tarry? Why are you so
helpless? If you know it not, seek from the hoopoe the way to
Solomon's palace.

There make your litanies, there utter your secrets and your
needs; Solomon indeed knows the speech of all the birds.

Speech is a wind, O slave, and distracts the heart; but he
commands it, "Gather together the scattered ones!"

8

Have you ever seen any lover who was satiated with this
passion? Have you ever seen any fish that had become satiated
with this sea?

Have you ever seen any image that was fleeing from the
engraver? Have you ever seen any Vāmiq asking pardon of
'Adhrā?

In separation, the lover is like a name empty of meaning; but
a meaning such as belovedness has no need of names.

You are the sea, I am a fish—hold me as you desire; show
compassion, exercise kingly power—without you, I remain alone.

5 Puissant emperor, what dearth of compassion is this then? The
moment you are not present, the fire rages so high.

If the fire beholds you, it withdraws to a corner; for whoever
plucks a rose from the fire, the fire bestows a lovely rose.

Without you, the world is a torment; may it not be without
you for a single instant; by your life I implore this, for life
without you is a torture and an agony to me.

Your image like a sultan was parading within my heart, even
as a Solomon entering the Temple of Jerusalem;

Thousands of lanterns sprang into flame, all the temple was
illumined; paradise and the Pool of Kauthar thronged with
Riḍwān and houris.

10 Exalted be God, exalted be God! Within heaven so many
moons! This tabernacle is full of houris, only they are hidden
from the eyes of the blind.

Splendid, happy bird that has found a dwelling in love! How
should any but the 'Anqā find place and lodging in Mount Qāf?

Splendid, lordly 'Anqā, Emperor Shams-i Tabrīz! For he is the
Sun neither of the east nor of the west, nor of any place.

9

How would it be, if my fair love should take my hand tomor-
row, hang his head through the window like the lovely-featured
moon?

If my life-augmenter enters, loosens my hands and feet?—For
my hands and feet too are bound fast by the hand of fixed
banishment.

Then I would say to him, "By your life I swear that without
you, O life of my soul, gay company makes me not happy,
neither does wine intoxicate me."

Then if he replies coquettishly, "Be gone! What do you want
of me? I fear that your melancholy may make me melancholic!"
—

5   I would bring sword and windingsheet and bow my neck as a
sacrificial offering, saying, "Your head is aching because of me;
strike deliberately!

You know that I desire not to live without you; better for me
is death than banishment, by God who brings the dead to life.

I never could believe that you would turn away from your
servant; I ever said, the words spoken by my enemies are lying
inventions.

You are my soul, and without my soul I know not how to live;
you are my eyes, and without you I have not a seeing eye."

Let go these words; minstrel, strike up an air; bring forward rebeck and tambourine, if you do not have a reed pipe.

IO

Today give in full measure that pure wine; strike in utter confusion this hasty wheel of heaven.

Even granted that the unseen bowl has come hidden from the eyes, it is not possible to conceal drunkenness and depravity.

Love, whose trade is joy, sweet of speech and sweet of thought, snatch now the veil from the face of that veiled king;

Auspicious one, that cries of exultation may arise from this side and that, ho, fill up, rosy of cheek, flagon and bowl.

5   If you do not wish the rosebower to be disclosed, why did you open the rosewater shop?

Having robbed us of our senses and set this river flowing, fling into the water with all speed the water-duckling.

O soul, we are as corn sprung in this expanse, dry of lip and seeking with our lives the cloud-borne rain.

On every side a new messenger declares, "You will never find; depart!" Cry "God forfend" against that ill-omened crow.

Riot-provoker of every spirit, purse-robber of every Goha, filching the rebeck from the hand of Bū Bakr the Lutanist,

10   Today I desire that you should intoxicate and craze this chatterbox soul, that wordy reason.

Water of life to us, become manifest as the resurrection, what though the milk of the scabby camel is life to the bedouin.

Very lovely is your majesty and beauty; be silent and hold your breath, make not aware of us every heedless one drowned in slumber.

II

Like the rose I am laughing with all my body, not only with my mouth, because I am without myself, alone with the king of the world.

You who came with torch and at dawn ravished my heart, dispatch my soul after my heart, do not seize my heart alone.

Do not in rage and envy make my soul a stranger to my heart; do not leave the former here, and do not summon the latter alone.

Send a royal message, issue a general invitation; how long, O sultan, shall the one be with you and the other alone?

5   If you do not come tonight as yesterday and close my lips, I will make a hundred uproars, my soul, I will not lament alone.

12

Come, you who have given new life to the world, put out of action cunning reason.

Until you flight me like an arrow, I cannot fly; come, fill once more the bow.

Because of your love, the bowl has fallen again from the roof; once more send down from the roof that ladder.

Men ask me, "In which direction is His roof?" In that direction whence the soul was brought;

5   In that direction whither every night the soul departs, then in the time of dawn He brings back the soul;

In that direction whence spring comes to the earth, and at dawn He bestows a new lamp upon the heavens;

In that direction whence a staff became a serpent, and He bore off Pharaoh's host to hell;

In that direction whence arose this quest in you—itself a token, it seeks a token.

You are that man who is seated upon an ass, and keeps asking of the ass this and that.

10   Be silent; for out of jealous regard He desires not to bring all and sundry into the sea.

13

Do you break our harp, exalted one; thousands of other harps are here.

Since we have fallen into the clutches of love, what matters it if we lose harp or reed pipe?

If the whole world's rebeck and harp should be consumed, many a hidden harp there is, my friend;

The twanging and strumming mounts to the skies, even if it does not enter the ears of the deaf.

5   If the whole world's lamp and candle should flicker out, what cause for sorrow is that, since flint and steel still remain?

Songs are spindrift on the face of the sea; no pearl comes on the surface of the sea;

Yet know that the grace of the spindrift derives from the pearl, the reflection of the reflection of whose gleam is upon us.

Songs are all but a branch of the yearning for union; branch and root are never comparable.

Close your lips, and open the window of the heart; by that way be conversant with the spirits.

14

O soul and stay of every soul, who bestow wings and set the spirits in motion,

With you, what fear have we of loss, you who convert all losses to gain?

Alas for the arrows of the glances and the brows curved like bows!

You have sugared the ruby lips of fair idols, you have opened those mouths in desire.

5   You who have put a key in our hand and therewith opened the door of the worlds,

If you be not in the midst of us, then why are those waists close-girdled?

And if yours is not the wine without token, of what are these tokens testimony?

And if you are beyond our surmise, yet through whom are these surmises living?

And if you are hidden from our world, from whom do the hidden things become manifest?

10   Let go the tales of this world; we have grown aweary of them.

The soul that has fallen into the sugar-sprinkler—how should such things be contained in its heart?

He who has become the earth for your feet, how should he be mindful of the heavens?

Bind up our tongue with your protection; cast us not forth into the midst of these tongues.

15

I beheld the lovely rosebower face, that eye and lamp of all brightness,

That altar before which the soul prostrates, that gladness and place of security.

The heart said, "I will yield up my soul there, I will let go of being and selfhood."

The soul also joined in the concert and began to clap hands.

5   Reason came and said, "What shall I say regarding this good fortune and sublime felicity,

This scent of a rose that made upright as a cypress every back that was curved and bent double?"

In love all things are transformed; Armenian is changed to Turk.

Soul, you have attained to the Soul of the soul; body, you have abandoned bodihood.

The ruby is the alms of our Beloved; the dervish eats the gold of the Rich;

10   That Mary in anguish discovers anew dates fresh and ripe.

Lest the eye of a stranger should fall upon it, do not show off your good deed to men;

If your desire from faith is security, seek your security in seclusion.

What is the place of seclusion? The house of the heart; become habituated to dwell in the heart;

In the heart's house is delivered that bowl of wholesome and everlasting wine.

15 Be silent, and practise the art of silence; let go all artful bragging;
For the heart is the place of faith, there in the heart hold fast to faithfulness.

16

Lover has rosebowers amid the veil of blood; lovers have affairs to transact with the beauty of incomparable Love.

Reason says, "The six directions are the boundary, and there is no way out"; Love says, "There is a way, and I have many times travelled it."

Reason beheld a bazaar, and began trading; Love has beheld many bazaars beyond Reason's bazaar.

Many a hidden Manṣūr there is who, confiding in the soul of Love, abandoned the pulpit and mounted the scaffold.

5 Dreg-sucking lovers possess ecstatic perceptions inwardly; men of reason, dark of heart, entertain denials within them.

Reason says, "Set not your foot down, for in the courtyard there is naught but thorns"; Love says, "These thorns belong to the reason which is within you."

Beware, be silent; pluck the thorn of being out of the heart's foot, that you may behold the rosebowers within you.

Shams-i Tabrīzī, you are the sun within the cloud of words; when your sun arose, all speech was obliterated.

17

Yesterday I gave a star a message for you; I said to it, "Deliver my compliments to that one fair as the moon."

Prostrating myself, I said, "Convey this prostration to that sun who by his burning glow converts hard rocks to gold."

I opened my breast and showed it the wounds; I said to it,

"Bear tidings of me to the Beloved who delights in drinking blood."

I rocked to and fro to hush the infant of my heart; the infant sleeps when the cradle is rocked.

5   Give milk to the infant of my heart, deliver us from turning about, you who every moment succour a hundred helpless ones like me.

After all, in the first place the heart's abode was the city of union; how long will you keep in exile this vagrant heart?

I have relapsed into silence; but to ward off crop-sickness turn about, O saki of the lovers, your vintner eye!

18

Go forth, my comrades, draw along our beloved, at last bring to me the fugitive idol;

With sweet melodies and golden pretexts draw to the house that moon sweet of presence.

And if he promises, "I will come in another moment," all his promises are but cunning to beguile you.

He possesses a flaming breath, by enchantment and wizardry knotting the water and tying up the air.

5   When in blessedness and joy my darling enters, sit you down and behold the marvels of God!

When his beauty shines forth, what shall be the beauty of the comely ones? For his sun-bright face extinguishes all lamps.

Go, fleet-paced heart, to Yemen, to my heart's beloved, convey my greetings and service to that ruby beyond price.

19

A garden—may its roses bloom till resurrection-day; an idol—may the two worlds be scattered over its beauty!

At daybreak the prince of the fair ones stalks forth to the

chase—may our hearts be the quarry for the arrows of his glances!

What messages are momently flashing from his eyes to mine —may my eyes be gladdened and intoxicated by his message!

I broke down the door of an ascetic; with an imprecation he banned me: "Be gone! May your days all be without peace!"

5   Thanks to his curse, the beloved has left me neither peace nor heart, that beloved who thirsts for my blood—may God befriend him!

My body is like the moon, melting away out of love; my heart is like Venus' harp—may its strings be snapped!

Regard not the moon's melting, Venus' broken estate; behold rather the sweetness of his sorrow—may it increase a thousand-fold!

What a bride is in the soul! Through the reflection of her face may the world be fresh and figured as the hands of the newly-wedded!

Regard not the fleshly cheek, which corrupts and decays; regard the spiritual cheek—may it be fair and lovely for ever!

10 The dark body is like a raven, and the physical world is winter —despite these two unlovelies, may there be spring eternal!

For these two unlovelies subsist through the four elements; may your servants subsist through other than these four!

20

When you display that rosy cheek, you set the stones a-spinning for joy.

Once again put forth your head from the veil, for the sake of the dumbstruck lovers,

That learning may lose the way, that the man of reason may break his science to pieces;

That water through your reflection may convert to a pearl, that fire may abandon warfare.

5   With your beauty, I desire not the moon, neither those two or three hanging little lanterns.

With your face, I do not call the ancient, rusty heavens a mirror.

You breathed, and created anew in another shape this narrow world.

In desire for his Mars-like eye, play, Venus, again that harp!

21

The heart is like a grain of corn, we are like a mill; how does the mill know why this turning?

The body is like a stone, and the water its thoughts; the stone says, "The water knows what is toward."

The water says, "Ask the miller, for it was he who flung this water down."

The miller says to you, "Bread-eater, if this does not turn, how shall the crumb-broth be?"

5   Much business is in the making; silence, ask God, that He may tell you.

22

Here someone is hidden; suppose not that you are alone. She has very sharp ears; do not open your tongue to evil.

That peri has taken lodging by the fountain of your heart; thereby every form of image has become manifest to you.

Wherever a fountain is, there is a place for peris; you must act cautiously there.

Since these five fountains of the senses are flowing over your body, know that it is by the superintendence of that fairy that sometimes they are stopped up, sometimes set flowing.

5   Know also that those five inward senses, such as imagination and conception, are likewise five fountains running towards the pasture.

Every fountain has two superintendents and fifty controllers; they disclose their forms to you in the time of burnishing.

The peris smite you if you are unmannerly, for this kind of famous peri is impetuous and shows no favour.

Determinism beguiles deliberation, saying, "Now leap into action"; its cunning has snatched the blanket from a hundred thousand such as we.

Behold the birds in the cage, behold the fishes in the net, behold the hearts lamenting on account of that knowing trickster.

10 Open not your eye surreptitiously on any idol out of treachery, lest that all-seeing prince cast you from his regard.

Several verses still remain, but this fountain has sunk into the ground; that will bubble up from the fountain when we leap up tomorrow.

23

Bring into motion your amber-scattering tress; bring into dancing the souls of the Sufis.

Sun, moon and stars dancing around the circle, we dancing in the midst—set that midst a-dancing.

Your grace minstrelwise with the smallest melody brings into the wheel the Sufi of heaven.

The breeze of spring comes hurrying, uttering a melody; it sets the world a-laughing, raises autumn from the dead.

5 Many a snake becomes a friend, rose partners thorn; the season of scattering largesse is come to the king of the orchard.

Every moment a perfume wafts from the garden like a message some whither, as if to say, "Cry welcome today to the friends!"

The orchard, departed into its secret heart, is speaking to you; do you depart into your own secret, that life may come to your soul,

That the lily's bud may open its secret to the cypress, that the tulip may bring good tidings to willow and judas-tree,

That the secret of every young shoot may emerge from the depths, the ascensionists having set up a ladder in the garden.

10 The songbirds and nightingales are seated in the branches, like the guardian enjoying his stipend from the treasury;

These leaves are like tongues, these fruits like hearts—when the hearts show their faces, they give worth to the tongue.

24

You who are my soul's repose in the time of pain, you who
are my spirit's treasure in the bitterness of poverty,

That which imagination never conceived, reason and under-
standing never perceived, has entered my soul from you; there-
fore to you alone I turn in worship.

Through your grace I gaze boldly upon eternal life; O king,
how should a perishing empire beguile me?

The melody of that person who brings me glad tidings of you,
even if it be in sleep, is better than all poets' songs to me.

5   In the genuflections of prayer your image, O king, is as
necessary and obligatory to me as the seven oft-repeated verses.

When unbelievers sin, you are all compassion and interces-
sion; to me you are the chief and leader of the stonyhearted.

If everlasting bounty should offer all kingdoms and place
before me every hidden treasure,

I would prostrate myself with all my soul and lay my face on
the earth, I would say, "Out of all these, the love of a certain one
for me!"

For me the time of union is eternal life, for in that moment no
time contains me.

10   Life is a vessel, and in it union is a pure wine; without you, of
what avail to me is the labour of the vessels?

Before this, twenty thousand desires were mine; in my passion
for him, not one single aspiration has remained to me.

Through the succour of his grace, I have become secure from
the Monarch of the Unseen saying to me, *Thou shalt not see me.*

The essence of the meaning of "He" my heart and soul has
filled; he is—even though he said he is not—the third and the
second to me.

Union with him transported my spirit; my body paid not
attention, though disengaged from the body he became visible to
me.

15   I have become old in grief for him; but when you name
Tabriz, all my youth returns.

25

Again the violet bent double has arrived beside the lily, again the ruby-clad rose is tearing her gown to shreds;
  Again our green-gowned ones have gaily arrived from beyond the world swift as the wind, drunken and stalking and joyous.
  The standard-bearing cypress went off and consumed autumn with rage, and from the mountaintop the sweet-featured anemone showed its face.
  The hyacinth said to the jasmine, "Peace be upon you"; the latter replied, "Upon you be peace; come, lad, into the meadow!"
5 A Sufi on every side, having attained some favour, clapping hands like the plane-tree, dancing like the zephyr;
  The bud, concealing its face like veiled ladies—the breeze draws aside its chaddur saying, "Unveil your face, good friend!"
  The friend is in this quarter of ours, water in this our stream; lotus in your finery, why are you athirst and pale?
  Sour-faced winter has departed, that joy-slayer has been slain; swift-footed jasmine, long may you live!
  The busy narcissus winked at the verdure; the verdure understood its words and said, "Yours is the command."
10 The clove said to the willow, "I am in hope of you"; the willow answered, "My bachelor apartment is your private chamber—welcome!"
  The apple said, "Orange, why are you puckered?" The orange replied, "I do not show myself off for fear of the evil eye."
  The ringdove came cooing, "Where is that friend?" The sweet-noted nightingale pointed him to the rose.
  Beside the world's springtide there is a secret spring; moon-cheeked and sweet of mouth, give wine, O saki!
  Moon rising in the shadows of darkness, the light of whose lamp vanquishes the sun at noon!
15 Several words yet remain unsaid, but it is unseasonably late; whatever was omitted in the night I will complete tomorrow.

26

If you are Love's lover and in quest of Love, take a sharp dagger and cut the throat of bashfulness.

Know that reputation is a great barrier in the path; what I say is disinterested—accept it with a tranquil mind.

Why did that madman work a thousand kinds of madness, that chosen wild one invent a thousand wiles?

Now he rent his robe, now he ran over the mountains, now he quaffed poison, now he elected annihilation;

5   Since the spider seized such huge prey, consider what prey the snare of *My Lord the Most High* will take!

Since the love of Lailā's face had all that worth, how will it be with *He carried His servant by night?*

Have you not seen the *Dīvāns* of Vīsa and Rāmīn? Have you not read the stories of Vāmiq and 'Adhrā?

You gather up your garment lest the water should wet it; you must dive a thousand times into the sea.

Love's path has proved all drunkenness and abasement, for the torrent flows downwards; how should it run upwards?

10   You will be as a bezel in the lovers' ring, if you are the ear-ringed slave of the king, my master;

Just as this earth is thrall to the sky, just as the body is thrall to the spirit.

Come, say, what loss did earth suffer from this bond? What kindnesses has not reason done to the members?

My son, it behoves not to beat the drum under a blanket; plant your flag like a brave warrior in the midst of the plain.

With your spirit's ear listen to the thousand tumults echoing in the green dome's air from the clamour of the passionate ones!

15   When the cords of your robe are loosened by Love's intoxication, behold then the angel's rapture, the houri's amazement!

How all the world trembles, on high and below, because of Love, which transcends all below and on high!

When the sun has arisen, where then remains night? When the army of grace has come, where then remains affliction?

I fell silent; Soul of the soul, do you speak, for every atom has grown articulate out of love for your face.

27

You have seized me by the ear—whither are you drawing me?
Declare what is in your heart, and what your purpose is.

Prince, what cauldron did you cook for me last night? God
knows what melancholy madness there is in Love!

Since the ears of heaven and earth and the stars are all in your
hand, whither are they going? Even to that place whither you
said, "Come!"

The rest you seized only by one ear, me you seized by two;
from the roots of each ear I say, "Long may you endure!"

5   When a slave grows old, his master sets him free; when I
became old, He enslaved me over again.

Shall not children rise up white of hair at the resurrection?
But your resurrection has turned the old men's hair black.

Since you bring the dead to life and make the old men young,
I have fallen silent, and occupy myself with prayer.

28

If you do not know Love, question the nights, ask of the pale
cheek and the dryness of the lips.

Just as the water relates about the stars and the moon, even so
the physical forms relate about intellect and spirit.

From Love the soul learns a thousand manners of culture, such
culture as cannot be found from schools.

Amongst a hundred persons, the lover stands out as plain as
the shining moon in heaven amid the stars.

5   The mind, though it be apprised of all the doctrines of the
sects, knows nothing and is bewildered by the doctrine of Love.

The man who has a heart like Khiḍar, who has quaffed the
water of life of Love—to such a one the most limpid fountains
are nothing worth.

Toil not in the garden; behold within the soul of the lover
Damascus and Ghūṭa, rosebowers and all Nairab.

What is Damascus? For that is a paradise full of angels and
houris; minds are amazed at those cheeks and rounded chins.

Its delectable wine does not produce vomiting and crop-sickness, the sweetness of its halva does not give rise to boils and fevers.

10   All men, from king to beggar, are in the tug of appetite; Love delivers the soul out of all appetites and desires.

What pride does Love take in its purchasers? What sort of a prop are foxes to the lion?

Upon the datepalm of the world I do not discover one ripe date, for all my teeth have been blunted by unripe dates.

Fly on the wings of Love in the air and to the skies, be exempt like the sun from the need of all riding-beasts.

Lovers' hearts do not experience loneliness like simples, they have no fear of severance and separation like compounds.

15   Providence chose Love for the sake of the souls, the Cause purchased Love out of all things caused.

Love's deputy entered the breast of the Cadi of Kāb, so that his heart should shy from giving judgment and such prattle.

What a world! What rare arrangement and ordering, that casts a thousand confusions into well-ordered things!

Beggar of Love, for all the joys that the world contains, reckon that Love is the gold-mine, and those things but gilded.

Love, you have filched my heart by trickery and cunning; you lied—God forfend!—but sweetly and charmingly.

20   I desire to mention you, Love, with gratitude; but I am distraught with you, and my thought and reason are confused.

Were I to praise Love in a hundred thousand languages, Love's beauty far surpasses all such stammerings.

29

Our desert has no bounds, our hearts and souls know no rest.

World upon world took shape and form; which of these shapes is ours?

When you see on the road a severed head which goes rolling towards our arena,

Ask of it, ask of it our secrets, for from it you will hear our hidden mystery.

How would it be, if but one ear showed itself, familiar with
the tongues of our birds?

How would it be if one bird took wing, having on its neck the
collar of our Solomon's secret?

What am I to say, what suppose? For this tale transcends our
bounds and possibilities.

Yet how shall I keep silence? For every moment this distrac-
tion of ours becomes yet more distraught.

What partridges and falcons are flying with wings outspread
amidst the air of our mountainland,

10 Amidst the air, which is the seventh atmosphere, on the sum-
mit whereof is our portico!

Leave this tale; ask not of us, for our tale is broken entirely;

Ṣalāḥ al-Ḥaqq wa'l-Dīn will display to you the beauty of our
Emperor and Ruler.

30

A hundred drums are being beaten within our hearts, the roar
of which we shall hear tomorrow.

Cotton wool in the ear, hair in the eye—that is the anxiety
for tomorrow, the subtle whisper of grief;

Fling Love's flame into this cotton wool, like Ḥallāj and like
the people of purity.

Why do you keep fire and cotton wool together? These two
are opposites, and the opposite never survived.

5 Since the encounter of Love is near, be joyous of presence for
the day of meeting.

For us, death is gladness and encounter; if for you it is an
occasion of mourning, depart hence!

Inasmuch as this present world is our prison, the ruining of
prisons is surely a cause for joy.

He whose prison was so delightful—how shall be the court of
Him who adorned the world?

Look not for constancy in this prison, for herein constancy
itself never kept faith.

3 1

Hark, for I am at the door! Open the door; to bar the door is not the sign of good pleasure.

In the heart of every atom is a courtyard for You; until You unbar it, it will remain in concealment.

You are the Splitter of Dawn, the Lord of the Daybreak; You open a hundred doors and say, "Come in!"

It is not I at the door, but You; grant access, open the door to Yourself.

5 Sulphur came to a fire; it said, "Come out to me, beloved!

My form is not your form, but I am all you, my form is as a veil.

I become you in form and reality when you arrive, my form is blotted out in the encounter."

The fire replied, "I have come forth; why should I veil my face from my very self?"

Hark, receive from me and deliver my message to all the companions and all the kinsmen.

10 If it is a mountain, draw it like a straw; I have given you the quality of amber.

My amber draws the mountain; did I not bring forth Mount Ḥirā out of nonexistence?

I am wholly and completely within your heart, for the pearl of the heart was born of my ocean.

I move my shadow, otherwise how is it that my shadow is apart from me?

15 But I transport it from its place so that, at the time of unveiling, its union may become manifest,

So that it may realize that it is a branch of me, so that it may become separated from all other.

Go to the saki and hear the rest of it, that he may tell you it with the tongue of immortality.

3 2

The wheel of heaven, with all its pomp and splendour, circles around God like a mill.

My soul, circumambulate around such a Kaaba; beggar, circle about such a table.

Travel like a ball around in His polo-field, inasmuch as you have become happy and helpless.

Your knight and rook are circumambulating about the king, even though you move from place to place on this chessboard.

He set on your finger the royal signet so that you might become a ruler having authority.

Whoever circumambulates about the heart becomes the soul of the world, heart-ravishing.

The heart-forlorn becomes companion to the moth, he circles about the tip of the candle,

Because his body is earthy and his heart of fire—congener has an inclination towards congener.

Every star circles about the sky, because purity is the congener of purity.

o The mystic's soul circles about annihilation, even as iron about a magnet,

Because annihilation is true existence in his sight, his eyes having been washed clean of squinting and error;

The drunkard made ablution in urine, saying, "O Lord, deliver me out of impurity."

God answered, "First realize what impurity is; it is not meet to pray crookedly and topsy-turvy.

For prayer is a key; and when the key is crooked, you will not attain the favour of opening the lock."

15 I fall silent; all of you, leap up! The cypress-like stature of my idol cries come!

Emperor of Tabriz, my King, Shams-i Dīn, I have closed my lips; do you come, and open!

33

The water has been cut off from this world's river; O spring-tide, return and bring back the water!—

Of that water whose like the fountain of Khiḍar and Ilyās never saw and will never see.

Glorious fountain, through the splendour of whose gushing every moment water bubbles up from the well of the soul.

When waters exist, loaves grow; but never, my soul, did water grow from loaf.

5   O guest, do not beggarlike shed the water from the face of poverty for the sake of a morsel of bread.

The entire world from end to end is but half a morsel; because of greed for half a morsel, the water vanished.

Earth and heaven are bucket and pitcher; water is outside earth and heaven.

Do you also speed forth from heaven and earth, that you may behold water flowing from placelessness,

That the fish of your soul may escape from this pool, and sip water from the boundless sea.

10   In that sea whose fishes are all Khiḍars, therein the fish is immortal, immortal the water.

From that vision came the light of the eye, from that roof is the water in the spout;

From that garden are these roses of the cheeks, from that waterwheel the rosebower obtains water;

From that date-tree are the dates of Mary. That water derives not from secondary causes and suchlike things.

Your soul and spirit will then become truly happy, when the water comes flowing towards you from hence.

15   Shake no more your rattle like a nightwatchman, for the water itself is the guardian of these fishes.

34

Do you not know what the rebeck says concerning tears of the eyes and burning hearts?

"I am a skin far sundered from the flesh; how should I not lament in separation and torment?"

The stick also says, "I was once a green branch; that cavalcade broke and tore to pieces my saddle."

We are exiles in separation; O kings, give ear to us—"To God is the returning."

5   From God in the first place we sprang in the world; to Him likewise we revert from the revolution.

Our cry is like the bell in the caravan, or as thunder when the clouds travel the sky.

Wayfarer, set not your heart upon a lodging-place, becoming weary at the time of attraction;

For you have departed from many a stage, from the sperm until the season of youth.

Take it lightly, that you may escape easily; give up readily, and so find the reward.

10 Take hold of Him firmly, for He has taken firm hold on you; first He and last He—go, discover Him.

Gently He draws the bow, for that arrow of His quivers in the hearts of the lovers.

Be the lover Turk or Greek or Arab, this cry right enough is fellow-tongue with him.

The wind is lamenting and calling to you, "Come in my wake, even to the river of water.

I was water; I became wind; I have come to deliver the thirsty ones from this mirage."

15 Speech is that wind which was formerly water; it becomes water when it casts off the veil.

This shout arose from without the six directions: "Flee from direction, and turn not your face from Us."

O lover, you are not less than the moth; when does the moth ever avoid the flame?

The King is in the city; for the sake of the owl how should I abandon the city and occupy the ruin?

If an ass has gone mad, strike the ox-whip upon its head until its senses return.

20 If I seek his heart, his worthlessness increases still more; God said regarding the unbelievers, *Strike their necks.*

35

That moon has returned, whose like the sky never saw even in dreams; he has brought a fire which no water can extinguish.

Behold the body's tenement, and behold my soul—Love's cup has intoxicated the one and ruined the other.

When the master of the tavern became my heart's companion, my blood turned to wine out of love, my heart to roast.

When the eye is filled with his image, a voice proclaims,
"Well done, goblet, and bravo, wine!"
5   My heart suddenly descried the ocean of Love; it leaped away
from me, saying, "Come, find me now!"
The sun of the countenance of Shams-i Dīn, Pride of Tabriz
—in its track like clouds all hearts are running.

36

You who possess not Love, it is lawful to you—sleep on; be
gone, for Love and Love's sorrow is our portion—sleep on.
We have become motes of the sun of sorrow for the Beloved;
you in whose heart this passion has never arisen, sleep on.
In endless quest of union with Him we hurry like a river; you
who are not anguished by the question "Where is He?"—sleep
on.
Love's path is outside the two and seventy sects; since your
love and way is mere trickery and hypocrisy, sleep on.
5   His dawn-cup is our sunrise, his crepuscule our supper; you
whose yearning is for viands and whose passion is for supper,
sleep on.
In quest of the philosopher's stone we are melting like copper;
you whose philosopher's stone is the bolster and the bedfellow,
sleep on.
Like a drunkard you are falling and rising on every side, for
night is past and now is the time for prayer; sleep on.
Since fate has barred slumber to me, young man, be gone; for
sleep has passed you by and you can now fulfil slumber; sleep on.
We have fallen into Love's hand—what will Love do? Since
you are in your own hand, depart to the right hand—sleep on.
10   I am the one who drinks blood; my soul, you are the one who
eats viands; since viands for a certainty demand slumber, sleep
on.
I have abandoned hope for my brain and my head too; you
aspire to a fresh and juicy brain—sleep on.
I have rent the garment of speech and let words go; you, who
are not naked, possess a robe—sleep on.

37

Since midnight sickness has manifested itself in that Master; till daybreak he has been beating his head uncontrollably against our wall.

Heaven and earth weep and lament because of his lamentation; his breaths have become fiery—you might say he is a fire-temple.

He has a strange sickness—no headache, no feverish pain—no remedy is to be found for it on earth, for it came upon him out of heaven.

When Galen beheld him he took his pulse; and he said, "Let go my hand and examine my heart; my pain is beyond the rules."

He suffers neither from yellow nor black bile, neither colic nor dropsy; a hundred tumults have arisen in every corner of our city because of this untoward happening.

He neither eats nor sleeps; he receives his nourishment from Love, for this Love is now both nurse and mother to the Master.

I said, "O God, grant compassion, that he may find rest for a brief hour; he has spilled no man's blood, he has seized no man's property."

The answer came from heaven, "Let him be as he is, for medicine and remedy are useless in lovers' suffering.

Seek no cure for this Master; do not bind him, do not counsel him, for where he has fallen is neither transgression nor piety. When did you ever see Love? You have never heard from lovers; keep silent, chant no spells; this is not a case for magic or jugglery!"

Come, Shams-i Tabrīzī, source of light and radiance, for this illustrious spirit without your splendour is frozen and congealed.

38

I have come so that, tugging your ear, I may draw you to me, unheart and unself you, plant you in my heart and soul.

Rosebush, I have come a sweet springtide unto you, to seize you very gently in my embrace and squeeze you.

I have come to adorn you in this worldly abode, to convey you above the skies like lovers' prayers.

I have come because you stole a kiss from an idol fair; give it back with a glad heart, master, for I will seize you back.

5   What is a mere rose? You are the All, you are the speaker of the command *Say*. If no one else knows you, since you are I, I know you.

You are my soul and spirit, you are my *Fātiḥa*-chanter; become altogether the *Fātiḥa*, so that I may chant you in my heart.

You are my quarry and game, though you have sprung from the snare; return back to the snare, and if you go not, I will drive you.

The lion said to me, "You are a wondrous deer; be gone! Why do you run in my wake so swiftly? I will tear you to pieces."

Accept my blow, and advance forward like a hero's shield; give your ear to naught but the bowstring, that I may bend you like a bow.

10 So many thousand stages there are from earth's bounds to man; I have brought you from city to city, I will not leave you by the roadside.

Say nothing, froth not, do not raise the lid of the cauldron; simmer well, and be patient, for I am cooking you.

No, for you are a lion's whelp hidden in a deer's body: I will cause you suddenly to transcend the deer's veil.

You are my ball, and you run in the curved mallet of my decree; though I am making you to run, I am still running in your track.

39

Come, come, for the rosebower has blossomed; come, come, for the beloved has arrived.

Bring at once altogether soul and world; deliver over to the sun, for the sun has drawn a fine blade.

Laugh at that ugly one showing off airs; weep for that friend who is severed from the Friend.

The whole city seethed when the rumour ran abroad that the madman had once again escaped from his chains.

5   What day is it, what day is it, such a day of uprising?—Per-

chance the scroll of men's deeds has already fluttered from the skies.

Beat the drums, and speak no more; what place is there for heart and mind? For the soul too has fled.

40

This house wherein continually rings the sound of the bell-staff—ask of the master what house this house is.

What is this idol-form, if it is the house of the Kaaba? And what is this light of God, if it is the Magian temple?

In this house is a treasure which the whole of being cannot contain; this house and this master are all a fiction and a pretence.

Lay not hand upon this house, for this house is a talisman; speak not to the master, for he is drunk since last night.

The dust and rubbish of this house is all ambergris and musk; the noise of the door of this house is all verse and melody.

In short, whoever enters this house has found a way to the King of the world, the Solomon of the time.

Master, bend down your head once from this roof, for in your fair face is the token of fortune.

I swear by your life that, but for beholding your countenance, though it be the kingdom of the earth, all is mere fantasy and fable.

The garden is baffled as to which is the leaf, which the blossom; the birds are distraught as to which is the snare, which the bait.

This is the Master of heaven, who is like unto Venus and the moon, and this is the house of Love, which is without bound and end.

The soul, like a mirror, has received your image in its heart; the heart has sunk like a comb into the tip of your tress.

Since in Joseph's presence the women cut their hands, come to me, my soul, for the Soul is there in the midst.

The whole household is drunk, and nobody is aware who enters the threshold, whether it be X or Y.

It is inauspicious; do not sit on the threshold, enter the house at once; he whose place is the threshold keeps all in darkness.

15 Though God's drunkards are thousands, yet they are one; the drunkards of lust are all double and treble.

Enter the lions' thicket and do not be anxious for the wounding, for the anxiety of fear is the figments of women;

For there no wounding is, there all is mercy and love, but your imagination is like a bolt behind the door.

Set not fire to the thicket, and keep silence, my heart; draw in your tongue, for your tongue is a flame.

41

Come, for today is for us a day of festival; henceforward joy and pleasure are on the increase.

Clap hands, say, "Today is all happiness"; from the beginning it was manifestly a fine day.

Who is there in this world like our Friend? Who has seen such a festival in a hundred cycles?

Earth and heaven are filled with sugar; in every direction sugarcane has sprouted.

5 The roar of that pearl-scattering sea has arrived; the world is full of waves, and the sea is invisible.

Muhammad has returned from the Ascension; Jesus has arrived from the fourth heaven.

Every coin which is not of this place is counterfeit; every wine which is not of the cup of the Soul is impure.

What a splendid assembly, where the saki is good fortune, and his companions are Junaid and Bā Yazīd!

Crop-sickness afflicted me when I was desirous; I did not know that God Himself desires us.

10 Now I have fallen asleep and stretched out my feet, since I have realised that good fortune has drawn me on.

42

In this river the heart is like a ruined waterwheel; in whichever direction it turns, there is water before it;

And even if you turn your back to the water, the water runs hurrying before you.

How shall the shadow save its soul from the sun, seeing that its soul is in the hand of the sun?

If the shadow stretches forth its neck, the sun's face that instant is shrouded.

Brave Sun, before which this sun in heaven quivers with fear like quicksilver!

The moon is like quicksilver on a palsied palm—one night only, and for the rest it is poured forth;

In every thirty nights, two nights it is united and lean, for the rest it endures separation, and separation is torture.

Though it is wretched, it is fresh of face; laughter is the habit and wont of lovers.

It lives laughing, and likewise dies laughing, for its return is to laughing fortune.

Keep silent, for the faults of vision always come from question and answer.

43

So long as the form of the Beloved's image is with us, for us the whole of life is a joyful parade.

Where friends unite together, there in the midst of the house, by Allah, is a spreading plain;

And where the heart's desire comes true, there one thorn is better than a thousand dates.

When we are sleeping at the head of the Beloved's lane, our pillow and blankets are the Pleiades;

When we are twisted into the tip of the Beloved's tress on the Night of Power, power belongs to us.

When the reflexion of His beauty shines forth, mountainland and earth are silk and brocade.

When we ask of the breeze the scent of Him, in the breeze is the echo of lute and reedpipe.

When we write His name in the dust, every particle of dust is a dark-eyed houri.

We chant a spell of Him over the fire; thereby the raging fire becomes water-cool.

10   Why shall I tell a long tale? For when we mention His name to nonbeing too, it increases being.

That subtlety in which Love is contained is fuller of pith than a thousand walnuts.

That instant when Love showed its face, all these things vanished from the midst.

Silence! For the sealing has been completed; the totality of desire is God Most High.

44

Today a new madness has arrived, it has dragged the chains of a thousand hearts;
Today it has rent the sides of the bags of white sugar candy.

Again that bedouin has purchased the Joseph of beauty for eighteen base pieces.

All night the souls in glory and felicity pastured amidst narcissus and jasmine,

5   Until with the dawn of course every spirit leaped forth nimble and sprightly.

Today narcissus-bed and anemone have blossomed out of stones and clods,

The tree has bloomed in the midst of winter, in January the fruits have ripened.

You might say that God has created a new world in this ancient world.

Lover-gnostic, recite this ode, for Love has chosen you out of all the lovers.

10   On your golden cheek there is a toothmark—has that silvery-breasted one perchance bitten you?

It is right that He should cherish that heart which has throbbed much in anguish for Him.

Silence! Go sauntering through the meadow for today it is the turn for the eyes to behold.

45

Which is the road by which I came? I would return, for it
likes me not here;
One moment's absence from the Beloved's lane is unlawful
according to the doctrine of lovers.
If only in all the village there is someone—by Allah, a sign
would be completely sufficient.
How shall the finch escape? For even the simurgh is footfast
in this stout snare.
My heart, do not come wandering in this direction; sit there,
for it is a pleasant station.
Choose that dessert which augments life, seek that wine which
is full-bodied;
The rest is all scent and image and colour, the rest is all war
and shame and opprobrium;
Be silent, and sit down, for you are drunk, and this is the edge
of the roof.

46

Be gathered together, comrades, for this is not the time to
sleep; by Allah, every comrade who sleeps is not of the true
companions.
Whoever is not turning about and weeping after the fashion
of a waterwheel shall not see the face of the garden, he will lose
the way to the garden.
You who have sought the heart's desire in the world of water
and clay, you are running towards that river in which there is no
water.
O moon, come forth from the heart's sky and turn our night to
day, that no night-traveller may say, "Tonight is not a night of
moonshine."
May my heart be unapprised of where the Beloved is, if my
heart is not quivering like the heart of quicksilver for the love of
Him.

47

Love resides not in science and learning, scrolls and pages; whatever men chatter about, that way is not the lovers' way.

Know that the branch of Love is in pre-eternity and its roots in post-eternity; this tree rests not upon heaven and earth, upon legs.

We have deposed reason and circumscribed passion, for such majesty is not appropriate to this reason and these habits.

So long as you are desirous, know that this desire of yours is an idol; when you have become beloved, after that there is no existence for the desirous.

5   The mariner is always upon the planks of fear and hope; once planks and mariner have passed away, nothing remains but drowning.

Shams-i Tabrīzī, you are at once sea and pearl, for your being entirely is naught but the secret of the Creator.

48

Mind you do not slip, for the road behind and ahead is wet with blood; man-robbers are nowadays more numerous than gold-robbers.

If they are intent on robbing people of reason and awareness, what then will they make of him who is unaware of himself?

Do not consider yourself's self so worthless and without antagonist; the world is in quest of gold, and your self is the mine of gold.

The prophet of God said, "Men are as mines"; the self is a mine of silver and gold and is truly full of gems.

5   You find a treasure, and therein you find not life for all the treasure; discover yourself, for this worldly treasure passes away from you.

Discover yourself, and be wary; yet what are you to do? For there is a wakeful, quickhanded thief on this way.

Though the dawn is dark, day is to be reckoned at hand; whoever's face is turned towards the sun is as the dawn.

The spirits become intoxicated through the breath of day-
break, inasmuch as the face of daybreak is towards the sun and is
the companion of vision.

You fling down the counter so many times upon "haply" and
"perchance," for you are very bankrupt, and heaven's wheel
carries off everything.

10   Brain-sieved and aware of nothing, you have fallen asleep—
one might say your morsel of daily bread is the brain of an ass.

Labour more, and collect gold, and be joyful, for all your
silver and gold and wealth is the serpent of hell.

For God's sake, live one night without eating and sleeping; a
hundred nights because of lust your carnal soul is sleepless and
foodless.

Out of agony and grief, from behind every atom of dust comes
sighing and lamentation, but your ear is deaf.

Sprinkle the heart's blood on your cheek at dawn, for your
provision for the way is heart's blood and the sigh of morn.

15   Fill your heart with hope, and polish it well and clear, for your
pure heart is the mirror of the sun of splendour.

Say, who is the companion of Aḥmad the Apostle in this
world? Shams-i Tabrīz the Emperor, who is *one of the greatest
things*.

49

Has perchance this instant the tip of that tress become scat-
tered? For such a Tartar musk has become amber-diffusing.

Has perchance the dawn breeze lifted the veil from His face?
For thousands of unseen moons have begun to shine.

Is there any soul which is not happy through His sweet
perfume? Though the soul has no clue as to the source of its
happiness.

Many a happy rose is laughing through the breath of God, yet
every soul does not know whence it has become laughing.

5   How fairly the sun of His cheek has shone today, through
which thousands of hearts have become rubies of Badakhshān.

Yet why should not the lover set his heart upon Him through
whose grace the body has become wholly soul?

Did the heart perchance one morning behold Him as He is, so that from that vision of Him it has today become after this wise?

Ever since the heart beheld that peri-born beauty of mine, it has taken the glass into its hand and become an exorcist.

If His sweet breeze blows upon the tree of the body, how a-tremble two hundred leaves and two hundred branches have become!

10   If there is not an immortal soul for every one slain by Him, why has it become so easy for the lover to yield up his soul?

Even the aware ones are unaware of His life and activities, for His life and activities have become their veil.

If the minstrel of Love has not breathed upon the reed of a heart, why has every tip of the hair become lamenting like the reed pipe?

If Shams-i Tabrīz does not fling clods from the roof against the heart, then why have the souls become as it were his doorkeepers?

50

He said, "Who is at the door?" I said, "Your humble slave."
He said, "What is your business?" I said, "Lord, to greet you."
He said, "How long will you drive?" I said, "Until you call."
He said, "How long will you boil?" I said, "Till the resurrection."
I laid claim to love, I swore many oaths that for love's sake I had lost kingship and nobility.
He said, "For a claim the cadi requires witness." I said, "My witness is my tears, my sign the pallor of my cheeks."
5   He said, "Your witness is invalid; your eye is wet-skirted." I said, "By the splendour of your justice, they are just and without fault."
He said, "Who was your companion?" I said, "Your fantasy, O King." He said, "Who summoned you hither?" I said, "The scent of your cup."
He said, "What is your intention?" I said, "Fidelity and friendship." He said, "What do you desire of me?" I said, "Your universal grace."
He said, "Where is it most agreeable?" I said, "Caesar's pal-

ace." He said, "What did you see there?" I said, "A hundred
miracles."
   He said, "Why is it desolate?" I said, "For fear of the highway-
man." He said, "Who is the highwayman?" I said, "This blame."
10 He said, "Where is safety?" I said, "In abstinence and godli-
ness." He said, "What is abstinence?" I said, "The way of salva-
tion."
   He said, "Where is calamity?" I said, "In the street of your
love." He said, "How fare you there?" I said, "In perfect recti-
tude."
   Silence! For if I were to utter his subtleties you would come
forth from yourself, neither door nor roof would remain to you.

51

   Show your face, for the orchard and rosegarden are my desire;
open your lips, for abundant sugar is my desire.
   Sun of beauty, come forth one moment out of the cloud, for
that glittering, glowing countenance is my desire.
   Out of your air I heard the sound of the falcon-drum; I
returned, for the sultan's forearm is my desire.
   You said capriciously, "Trouble me no more; be gone!" That
saying of yours, "Trouble me no more," is my desire,
5 And your repulse, "Be gone, the king is not at home," and
those mighty airs and brusqueness of the doorkeeper, are my
desire.
   In the hand of every one who exists there are filings of beauty;
that quarry of elegance and that mine are my desire.
   This bread and water of heaven's wheel are like a treacherous
torrent; I am a fish, a leviathan, Oman is my desire.
   Like Jacob I am crying alas, alas; the fair visage of Joseph of
Canaan is my desire.
   By Allah, without you the city is a prison for me; I wander
abroad, mountain and desert are my desire.
10 My heart is weary of these weak-spirited fellow-travellers; the
Lion of God and Rustam-i Dastān are my desire.
   My soul is sick of Pharaoh and his tyranny; that light of the
countenance of Moses son of 'Imrăn is my desire.

I am aweary of these tearful people so full of complaining; that ranting and roaring of the drunkards is my desire.

I am more eloquent than the nightingale, but because of vulgar envy a seal is on my tongue, and lamentation is my desire.

Last night the shaikh went all about the city, lamp in hand, crying, "I am weary of beast and devil, a man is my desire."

15 They said, "He is not to be found, we too have searched." He answered, "He who is not to be found is my desire."

Though I am penniless, I will not accept a small carnelian, for that rare, precious carnelian is my desire.

Hidden from every eye, and all things seen are from Him— that hidden One manifest in works is my desire.

My state has gone beyond every desire and yearning; from mine and place to the elements is my desire.

My ear heard the tale of faith and became drunk; where is the portion of sight? The form of faith is my desire.

20 In one hand the winecup, in the other the Beloved's curl—to dance so in the midst of the arena is my desire.

That rebeck says, "I am dead of expectation; the hand and bosom and plectrum of 'Uthmān are my desire."

I am at once Love's rebeck, and Love is my rebeck-player; those favours of the plucking of the All-merciful are my desire.

Cunning minstrel, number the rest of this ode after this fashion, for it is after this fashion I desire.

Show your face from the east, Sun of the Pride of Tabriz; I am the hoopoe, the presence of Solomon is my desire.

52

Though from left and right there is useless criticism and vilification, that man who has lost his heart turns not away from Love.

The moon scatters light, and the dog barks at it; what harm does that do to the moon? Such is a dog's speciality.

The lover is a mountain, not a straw to be blown away by the wind; it is a flock of flies that the wind has waylaid.

If it is the rule that blame should arise from Love, it is also the rule for Love to be deaf to it.

5   Desolation of both worlds on this road is true cultivation; to
eschew all benefits is a benefit in Love.
    Jesus from the fourth sphere calls, "Welcome! Wash your
hands and mouth, for now is the time for the Table."
    Go, become effaced in the Friend in the tavern of not-being;
wherever two drunkards are together, there is bound to be a
brawl.,
    You enter the devil's court crying, "Justice, justice!" Seek
justice from God, for here is nothing but wild beasts.
    The Prophet said, "Take not counsel from a woman"; this
carnal soul of ours is a woman, even though it be an abstinent.
10   Drink so much wine that you cease to chatter; after all, are
you not a lover? And is not this love a tavern?
    Though you should utter verse and prose like Ja'farī gold,
there where Ja'far is it is all worthless tales.

53

    My soul, spiritual beauty is passing fair and glorious, yet your
own beauty and loveliness is something beside.
    You who spend years describing spirit, show one quality that is
equal to his essence.
    Through his phantasm the light of the eye increases, yet for all
that in the presence of union with him it is clouded.
    I stand open-mouthed in reverence for that beauty; every
moment "God is greater" is on my tongue and in my heart.
5   The heart has acquired an eye constant in desire of you; ah,
how that desire nourishes the heart and eye!
    Speak not of houris and moon, spirit and peri, for these
resemble Him not; He is something other.
    Slave-caressing it is that your love has practised, else where is
the heart that is worthy of that love?
    Every heart that has been sleepless for one night in desire for
you is bright as day, and the air by it is illumined.
    Every one who has become without object is as your disciple;
his object is realized without the form of object.
10   Every limb of hell who has burned and fallen into this love,
has fallen into Kauthar, for your love is Kauthar.

My foot does not reach the ground out of hope for union, withal through separation from you my hand is on my head.

My heart, be not sorrowful at this oppression of foes, and meditate on this, that the Sweetheart is judge.

If my enemy is glad because of my saffron-pale face, is not my saffron-pale face derived from the red rose?

Since my Beloved's beauty surpasses description, how fat is my grief, and how lean my praise!

15   Yes, since it is the rule that the more the pain of the wretched sufferer is, the less is his lament.

Shams-i Dīn shone moonlike from Tabriz; no, what is the moon indeed? That face outshines the moon.

54

That spirit which wears not true love as a garment is better not to have been; its being is nothing but a disgrace.

Be drunk in love, for love is all that exists; without the commerce of love there is no admittance to the Beloved.

They say, "What is love?" Say, "The abandonment of free will." He who has not escaped out of free will, no free will has he.

The lover is an emperor; the two worlds are scattered over him; the king pays no heed to the scattering.

5   Love it is and the lover that remain till all eternity; set not your heart on aught but this, for it is merely borrowed.

How long will you embrace a dead beloved? Embrace the soul which naught embraces.

What was born of spring dies in the season of autumn; love's rosebower receives no replenishment from spring.

The rose that comes of spring, the thorn is its companion; the wine that comes of pressed grapes is not exempt from crop-sickness.

Be not an expectant spectator on this path; for by Allah, there is no death worse than expectancy.

10   Set your heart on the true coin, if you are not counterfeit; give ear to this subtlety, if you lack an earring.

Tremble not on the body's steed; fare lighter afoot; God gives
wings to him who rides not on the body.

Let go care and become wholly clear of heart, like the face of a
mirror without image and picture—

When it has become clear of images, all images are contained
in it; that clear-faced one is not ashamed of any man's face.

Would you have your self clear of blemish? Gaze upon Him,
for He is not ashamed or afraid of the truth.

15 Since the steely face gained this skill from purity, what shall
the heart's face, which is without dust, discover?

I said, "What shall it discover?" No, I will not say; silence is
better, lest the heart-ravisher should say, "He cannot keep a
secret."

55

Every moment the voice of Love is arriving from left and
right; we are departing for the skies—who has a mind for
sightseeing?

We were once in heaven, we were friends of the angels; let us
all return thither, for that is our city.

We are even higher than the heavens, we are greater than
angels; why should we not transcend both? Our lodging-place is
Majesty.

How far is the world of dust from the pure substance! Upon
what have you alighted? Load up—what place is this?

5 Young luck is our friend, to yield up the soul is our business;
the leader of our caravan is Muṣṭafā, Pride of the World.

At his moon the moon was split, it could not endure to behold
him; the moon attained such luck—she, a humble beggar.

The sweet scent of the breeze is from the curl of his tress, the
glitter of this phantasm is from that cheek like the forenoon.

Behold in our hearts every moment a splitting of the moon,
for why does your eye soar beyond the vision of that vision?

Mankind, like waterfowl, are sprung from the sea of the soul;
how should the bird that has risen from that sea make its
dwelling here?

10   Nay rather, we are pearls in that sea, we are all present therein; else, why does wave upon wave surge from the sea of the heart?

The wave of Alast came along and caulked the body's ship; when the ship is wrecked once more, the turn of union and encounter will come.

56

My being is but a goblet in the Beloved's hand—look at my eyes, if you do not believe it.

I am like a goblet, heart full of blood and body slender, in the hand of Love, which is neither pale nor lean nor slender.

This Love consumes nothing but Moslem blood; come, I will tell it in your ear—amazing, it is not an infidel.

A thousand forms like Adam and Eve are born; the world is full of His image, but He is not endowed with form.

5   He knows what is salutary for the desert sand-grain and the drop of the ocean, and brings replenishment, for His knowledge is not deaf.

Every moment He binds and releases our hearts; why should the heart not know Him by His actions, if it is not an ass?

Through being bound and released by the hand of the ass-driver the ass has become a gnostic, and knows that he is, and none beside;

Seeing him, it moves its head and ear assishly; it recognises his call, for it is not disguised.

From his hand it has consumed sweet provender and water—amazing! Do you not receive such provision from God?

10   A thousand times He has fettered you in pain, and you have cried out; why do you disapprove? God is not constrained to release you.

Like the infidel you bow your head only in time of affliction; not worth half a grain is the head that belongs not yonder.

A thousand spiritual forms are flying in the air like Ja'far-i Ṭaiyār, although they are not Ja'far;

But how should the cage-bird know about the air? It supposes gloomily, "I have no wings."

Every moment it puts its head out of the fissure of the cage; there is room for its head, but not its body, for the head is not the whole.

15   The fissure of your five senses is the fissure of that cage; you see a thousand prospects, but there is no way to the prospect.

Your body is dry tinder, and that vision is fire; when you look well into the matter, all is nothing but flame.

Not tinder is it, for it has become fire in burning; know that the tinder is light, although it is not shining.

For the sake of the ears of those who shall come after me I speak and set down; our life is not postponed;

For Love has seized them by the ear and is bringing them by secret ways where reason is no guide.

20   Muhammad's eye has closed in sleep, and the rebeck has become feeble; sleep not—these words are a treasure of gold, even if they are not gold in truth.

Mankind are stars, and Shams-i Tabrīzī is the sun; which star is there that is not illumined by his sun?

57

What pearl are you? For in no man's hand is the price of you. What does the world possess that is not your gift?

Is there a worse punishment than his who lives exiled from your face? Do not punish your servant, for all that he is unworthy of you.

Every moment I would scatter my heart and soul in your dust; dust be on the head of the soul that is not the dust of your feet!

Blessed to all birds is your air; how unblest is the bird that is not in your air!

5   Amidst the billows of contingencies even the master shall not escape by swimming, if he is not familiar with you.

The world has no permanence, and if it has, count it as perishing, since it is not intimate with your permanence.

How happy is the king that is mated by your rook! How fair of presence is he who is never without your presence!

I will not flee from your blow, for very raw indeed is the heart that is not roasted in the fire of your trial.

The heart that has not been naughted turns its face to place; from placelessness you drive it, saying, "Begone! This is no place for you."

10 There is no end to your praise and praisers; what atom is there that is not reeling with your praise?

As Niẓāmī expresses it in verse, "Tyrannise not, for I cannot endure your tyranny."

58

Three days it is now since my fair one has become changed; sugar is never bitter—how is it that that sugar is sour?

I dipped my pitcher into the fountain that contained the Water of Life, and I saw that the fountain was full of blood.

In the garden where two hundred thousand roses grew, in place of fruit and blossom there are thorns and stones and desert.

I chant a spell and whisper it over the face of that peri—for incantation is always the business of the exorcist—

5 Yet for all my incantations my peri came not back into the bottle, since his activities transcend chants and spells.

Between his brow there are ancient angers; the frown on the brow of Lailā is destruction to Majnūn.

Come, come, for without you I have no life; see, see, for without you my eyes are a veritable flood.

By the right of your moonlike countenance, brighten my eye, though my sins are greater than the whole of mankind's.

My heart turns about itself, saying, "What is my sin? For every cause is conjoined with a consequence."

10 A proclamation comes to me from the Marshal of eternal judgment: "Seek not about your own self, for this cause belongs not to now."

God gives and seizes, brings and carries away; His business is not to be measured by reason's scales.

Come, come, for even now by the grace of *Be and it is* paradise opens its gate which is *ungrudging*.

Of the essence of the thorn you behold marvellous flowers; of the essence of the stone you see the treasure of Korah.

Divine grace is eternal, and thereof a thousand keys lie hidden between the *kāf* and the ship of the *nūn*.

59

Love is nothing but felicity and lovingkindness, it is nothing but gladness and right guidance.

Bū Ḥanīfa did not teach love, Shāfi'ī had no tradition concerning it.

"Licit" and "illicit" operate till death; there is no terminus to the science of lovers.

Lovers are drowned in sugar-water; Egypt has nothing to complain about sugar.

5 How should the drunkard's soul not utter thanks for a wine to which there is no boundary and limit?

Whomsoever you have seen sorrowful and scowling is not a lover, and belongs not to that province;

Otherwise, every bud is a veil of a garden, jealousy and envy have no contagion.

The beginner in this path of Love is he who is not apprised of beginning.

Become naughted from selfhood, because there is no sin worse than being.

10 Do not be a shepherd, be a flock; shepherdry is nothing but a bar to providential care.

God is sufficient for many a servant's ill, but the servant has not this knowledge and sufficiency.

He says, "This is problematic and allegorical"; this is clear, this is not allegory.

A blind man struck his foot against a pitcher; he said, "The doorkeeper is not careful.

What are pitchers and glasses doing on the footpath? The road is not clear of these pots.

15 Remove the pitchers from the path; the doorkeeper is not attending to his job."

The doorkeeper answered, "Blind man, no pitcher is on the path, the fact is that you have no knowledge of the path.

You have left the path and are going to the pitcher; that is plain error."

Master, your drunkenness in the way of religion is the only sign from beginning to end.

You are a sign, and a seeker after a sign; there is no better sign than the seeker after a sign.

20 You are astray from the path, otherwise in the path of striving
no striver goes without his wages.

Just as *an atom's weight he shall see it*, an atom's weight of
slipping goes not unpunished;

An atom of good is not without a reward—open your eyes, if
you are not blind.

Every herb is a token of water; what is there that is not
tributary to that?

Enough, this water has many tokens; the thirsty man requires
no counselling.

60

The bird of my heart has again begun to flutter, the parrot
of my soul has begun to chew sugar.

My mad and drunken camel has begun to rend the chain of
reason.

A gulp of that incautious wine has begun to flow over my
head and eyes.

The lion of the gaze, despite the dog of the Companions of
the Cave, has begun to drink my blood again.

5   The water is flowing again in this river; by the riverbank
the grass has begun to shoot.

The dawn breeze is blowing again in the garden, it has
begun to blow over rose and rosebed.

Love sold me for a single fault; Love's heart burned, and
has begun to buy back.

He drove me away; compassion came to him and called;
Love has begun to look kindly upon me.

My enemy has seen that I am with the Friend; he has begun
to gnaw his hand of envy.

10   My heart has escaped from the trickery of fortune, it has
begun to creep into Love's bosom.

The tale-bearer brow making hints has begun to curve over
that eye.

When Love called my heart towards Him, my heart began
to flee from all creation.

Creatures are sticks; the blind man flings away the stick when he begins to see.

Creatures are like milk; the infant turns from milk when it has begun to digest viands.

15 The spirit is like a falcon taking wing, for it has begun to hear the drum of the king.

Enough, for the veil of speech has begun to spin a curtain around you.

61

The hour is late, the hour is late, the sun has gone down into the well, the sun of the soul of lovers has entered the seclusion of God.

A day is hidden in night, a Turk is amongst Hindus; night, launch your assaults, for that Turk is in the tent.

If you catch a glimpse of this brightness, you will set sleep afire; for by night-faring and servitude Venus became the companion of the moon.

We are fleeing by night and running apace, and the Zangis are on our track, for we carried off the gold, and the watchman became aware.

5 We have learned nightfaring and consumed a hundred watchmen; our cheeks are lit up like candles because that pawn of ours has become king.

Happy indeed is that smiling one who has pressed cheek against that cheek! Great and glorious is that heart which has departed unto that Sweetheart!

Who is there on the path of the heart who has not a sigh in his heart? That man is truly successful who is drowned in that sigh.

When he is drowned in the sea, the sea carries him up to the surface, like Joseph of the well who emerged from the well to greatness.

They say, "Man's origin is the dust, and he returns to the dust." How should he become dust who is the dust of this doorway?

10 The crops appear all of one kind until the harvest-time

arrives; one half of it has become fine grain, the other half is chaff.

62

Fair ones, fair ones, a fair one has gone mad; his bowl has fallen from the roof, he has gone to the madhouse.

He circled about the pool like men athirst seeking and searching; suddenly like a dry crust he became a sop in our pool.

Learned man, stop up your ears against this; do not listen to this incantation, for he has become a legend through our charm.

The ears do not escape from this ring which has robbed minds of their reason; having laid his head on the millstone, he vanished like a grain into the measure.

5   Regard it not as a sport, regard it not as a sport; here choose gambling away life; heads in plenty through love of his curls have become turned upside down like a comb.

Be not puffed up by your reason; many a well-trusted master who was a pillar of the world has become more lamenting than the Moaning Pillar.

I, who have cut away from life, roselike have rent my robe, thence have become such that my reason has become a stranger to my soul.

Those drops of individual reason have become vanquished in the Sea of Reason; the atoms of these fragmentary souls have become annihilated in the Beloved.

I will keep silent, I will perform the command and hide this candle—a candle in whose light the sun and the moon are moths.

63

Who is that, who is that who makes the breast sorrowful, then when you make complaint before Him, He turns your bitter sweet?

First He appears as a deaf adder, lastly He is a treasure of pearls. Sweet King, who in a moment transforms that bitterness to goodness!

Let it be a demon, He makes it into a houri, let it be a funeral, He makes it into a marriage-feast; and He makes knowing and world-beholding one blind from his mother's womb.

He makes the dark bright, He makes the thorn into a rosebud; He draws the thorn out of your palm, and fashions you a pillow of roses.

5 For the sake of Abraham His friend He causes the fire to flame, and converts Nimrod's furnace into blossoms and eglantine.

He who gives light to the stars and succour to the helpless, He benefits His servant, and too applauds His servant.

He causes all the sins of the sinners to scatter like December leaves; into the ears of those who speak Him ill He recites forgiveness of sin.

He says, "Say, O Faithful One, pardon the sin of one who slipped"; when a servant enters upon prayer, He secretly says Amen.

It is His amen which gives a man joy in his prayer; like a fig, He is inwardly and outwardly alike sweet and pleasant.

10 It is rapture which in good and evil gives strength to hand and foot, for this rapture mates the strength of a Rustam to the body of a poor wretch.

With rapture the poor wretch is a Rustam, without rapture Rustam is one full of grief; but for rapture, how would the Friend of the Soul stablish the soul?

I sent forth my heart timely (for it knows swiftly to travel the way), to carry the description of Shams-i Dīn to the Tabriz of fidelity.

64

Advice from anyone is never of profit to lovers; love is not the kind of torrent that anyone can dam up.

No man of intellect will ever know the head's ecstasy of the drunkard; no man of reason will ever know the heart's rapture of the reason-lost.

Kings would become indifferent to kingship if they caught a whiff of those wines which lovers drink in the heart's assembly.

Khusrau bids farewell to his kingdom for the sake of Shīrīn; Farhād too for her sake strikes the axe against the mountain.

5 Majnūn flees from the circle of men of intellect for love of Lailā; Vāmiq laughed at the mustachios of every puffed-up man.

Frozen is the life that has passed without that sweet spirit; rotten is the kernel that is oblivious of this almond-cake.

If yonder heaven were not spinning bewildered and in love like us, it would grow weary of its revolving, and say, "It is enough for me; how long, how long?"

The world is like a reed pipe, and He blows in its every hole; truly its every lament derives from those two sugar-sweet lips.

Behold how, when He blows into every clod, every heart, He bestows a need, He bestows a passion which raises lamentation of anguish.

10 If you tear the heart away from God, to whom will you then commit it? Tell me this. Soulless is the person who has been able to tear his heart away from God for a single moment.

I will make enough; go you nimbly, by night climb on to this roof; raise a fair clamour in the city, my soul, with a loud voice!

65

The springtide of lovers has come, that this dust bowl may become a garden; the proclamation of heaven has come, that the bird of the soul may rise in flight.

The sea becomes full of pearls, the salt marsh becomes sweet as Kauthar, the stone becomes a ruby from the mine, the body becomes wholly soul.

If the eyes and souls of lovers are raining a flood like a cloud, yet the heart within the body's cloud is flashing like lightning.

Do you know why the lovers' eyes have become like a cloud in Love? Because that moon generally is concealed in clouds. Happy and laughing hour, when those clouds have begun to weep! Lord, what a blessed state, when those lightnings are laughing!

Of those hundreds of thousands of drops, not one drop falls upon the earth; for if it should fall upon the earth, the whole world would be laid in ruin.

Though the whole world be laid in ruin, yet every desolation through love becomes fellow-mariner with Noah, and so is intimate with the Flood.

Did the flood abate, the heavens would not go round; through that wave beyond direction these six directions keep in motion.

You who remain fast under these six directions, at once sorrow and do not sorrow, for those seeds beneath the ground will one day become a plantation of date-trees.

One day that root will raise its head from the dust, it will become a fresh green branch; what if two or three branches should wither, the rest of the tree will be pregnant with life;

And when that dry branch is set afire, the fire will be joyous like the soul; if that is not this, it will become this; if this is not that, it will become that.

Something has closed my mouth, as if to say, "What, drunk and on the edge of the roof? Whatever it may be that bewilders you, that thing is bewildered at Him."

66

My Beloved leaves me not so much as to scratch my own head; it is the body of my Beloved that presses me in its breast.

Now He draws me in His train like a string of camels, anon the King places me in front like the commander of His troops.

Anon He sucks me like a seal-ring, to plant His seal through me; anon He makes me into a ring and fastens me on His door.

He takes blood and makes a sperm, He takes sperm and

fashions a creature; He slays the creature and fashions Reason, He makes manifest the resurrection.

5   Now He drives me away with a reed like a dove from the house, anon with a hundred entreaties He calls me to His presence.

Now He carries me like a ship on a voyage over the sea, anon He halts me and ties me to His own anchor.

Now He makes me water for the sake of the seeker after purity, anon He makes me a thorn in the path of His luckless ones.

The eternal eight paradises did not become the prospect of that King; how happy is this heart of mine, which He makes His prospect!

Not by the attestation of faith did I become a believer in that Beauty of the Soul; only then did I become a believer in It when I became an unbeliever in myself.

10   Whoever joined His ranks became secure from destruction by Him; I saw the sword in His hand, I burned that shield of mine.

I was like-pinioned with Gabriel, I had six hundred wings; now that I have reached Him, what shall I do with my wings?

Many days and nights I was guardian of the pearl of my soul; now in the current of the ocean of pearls I am indifferent to my own pearl.

How long will you essay to describe Him? For He comes not within description; make enough, that I may ride over my commotion.

67

The Friend is toggling me like a camel; in what train is He dragging His drunken camel?

He wounded my soul and body, He broke my glass, He bound my neck—to what task is He drawing me?

His net is carrying me like a fish to the shore; His snare is drawing my heart towards the Master of the chase.

He who makes the train of clouds, like camels under the

sky, to water the plain, is drawing me over mountain and cavern.

The thunder beats its drum; particle and whole have become alive; the scent of spring is wafting in the twig's heart and the marrow of the rose.

He who makes the recesses of the seed to be the cause of the fruit, He is dragging the secret of the tree's heart up to the gallows.

The grace of springtide breaks the pain of the garden's crop-sickness, even though the cruelty of winter is still drawing towards crop-sickness.

68

My heart, be seated near that person who has experience of the heart, go under that tree which bears fresh blossoms.

Go not in every direction as do idlers in this druggists' market; sit in the shop of someone who has sugar in his shop.

If you have no balance, then every one waylays you; one man adorns a counterfeit coin, and you imagine that he has gold;

Cheatingly he sets you by the door, saying, "I am coming" —do not sit expectant at the door, for that house has two doors.

Do not bring your cup to every pot that seethes, and do not sit there, for every seething pot has within it something else.

Not every reed holds sugar; not every under has an over; not every eye has sight; not every sea holds pearls.

Lament, singing nightingale, because the drunkard's lament has some effect, some effect even on rocks and stones.

Put aside your head if you have no room, for if the thread is not contained in the eye of the needle that is because it has a head.

This wakeful heart is a lantern; hold it under your skirt; pass away from this wind and air, for the air puts it into commotion.

When you have passed away from the wind you have

become a dweller in a fountain, you have become companion to a confederate who pours cooling water on the heart.

When you have water on your heart, you are like a green tree which constantly yields new fruit, and journeys within the Heart.

69

A fair idol that all the night teaches tricks to Venus and the moon, his two eyes by witchery sew up the two eyes of heaven.

Look out for your hearts, Moslems, for I at all events am so commingled with Him that no heart is commingled with me.

First I was born of His love, finally I gave my heart to Him; when fruit is born of a branch, from that branch it hangs.

I am fleeing from my own shadow, for the light is hidden from the shadow; where shall he rest at last who flees from his shadow?

5   The tip of His tress is saying, "Ha, quick, to the rope-trick!" The cheek of His candle is saying, "Where is the moth, that it may burn?"

For the sake of that rope-trick be brave, and become a hoop; fling yourself into the fire, when His candle is kindled.

When you have seen the joy of burning you will no more endure without the flame; even if the water of life came to you, it would not stir you from the flame.

70

My heart is like an oyster shell, the Beloved's phantom is the pearl; now I am no more contained, for this house is filled with Him.

Night split the lip of my soul with the sweetness of His talk; I am surprised at him who says, "Truth is bitter."

Mortals' food comes from without, but the lover's food is from within; he regurgitates and chews, for the lover is like a camel.

Be swift-faring like a peri, denude yourself of your body; nakedness is not allowed to him who has the mange.

Ṣalāḥ al-Dīn has come to the chase; all the lions are his quarry; that man is his servant who is free from the two worlds.

71

Once again the drunkards' head from drunkenness has come into prostration; has perchance that minstrel of the souls struck up music from the veil?

The reckless gamblers of head and soul once more are rioting; being has departed into annihilation, and annihilation has come into being.

Once more the world is full of the sound of Seraphiel's trumpet; the trustee of the unseen has become visible, for goods and chattels have come to the soul.

See how the earthy particles have received fresh life; all their earthiness has turned to purity, all their loss become gain.

That world is without colour; yet out of the crucible of the sight, like light, this red and blue have issued from the colour-mixing soul.

The body's portion of this is colour, the soul's portion is delight; for the cauldron's portion from the kitchen fire is smoke.

Consume, O heart, for so long as you are raw, the scent of the Heart will not come from you; when did you ever know anyone to produce the scent of incense without fire?

The scent is always with the incense, it never departed or returned thither; one man says, "It came late," another says, "It came early."

The Emperor has not fled from the ranks, only the helmet and armour are a veil; the veil over his moonlike face is a helmet against the blows of mortals.

72

The month of December has departed, and January too; come, for the spring has come, the earth is green and joyous, the time of the tulips has come.

See how the trees stagger and shake their hands as if drunk! The zephyr has recited a spell, so that the rosebower cannot rest.

The nenuphar said to the jasmine, "See how twisted together I am!" The blossoms said to the meadow, "The grace of the Omnipotent has descended."

The violet genuflected when the hyacinth bowed humbly, when the narcissus gave a wink, saying, "A time for taking note has come."

5   What did the tossing willow say, that it became light-headed with drunkenness? What did that fair-statured cypress behold, that it departed and returned firm of foot?

The painters have taken the brush, with whose hands my soul is intoxicated, for their lovely imageries have lent beauty to the grove.

Thousands of sweet-feathered birds seated on their pulpits are praising and reciting lauds, that the time of divulging has come.

When the soul's bird says "Yā Hū!" the ringdove replies "Where, where?" The former says, "Since you have not caught the scent, your portion is waiting."

The roses are bidden to show their hearts; it is not seemly to hide the heart, when the unveiling of the friend of the cave has come.

10   The rose said to the nightingale, "Look at the green lily— though it has a hundred tongues, it is steadfast and keeps its secret."

The nightingale replied, "Go forth, be busy disclosing my secret, for this love which I possess is reckless like you."

The plane-tree lowered its face to the vine—"Prostrate one, stand up!" The vine answered, "This prostrating of mine is not voluntary.

I am pregnant with that draught which smites at the drunk-ards; my inward is as fire, your outward is mere plane."

The saffron came forth gay, the mark of lovers on its cheek; the rose pitied it and said, "Ah, this poor creature, how abject it is!"

15 This encounter reached the ears of the laughing-faced, ruby apple, which said to the rose, "It knows not that the Beloved is longsuffering."

When the apple advanced this claim, that "I think well of the Lord," to put it to the proof stones rained from every side.

Someone stoned him; if he was a true lover, he laughs; why should not Shīrīn laugh when pelted by Khusrau?

The throwing of clods by the fair ones is meant for calling the lover; the cruelty of lovers to one another is not a sign of aversion.

If Zulaikhā that moment tore Joseph's shirt and collar, know that it was in sport and play that she unveiled his secret.

20 The apple absorbs the blow and comes not down, saying, "I am happy hanging here, for this honour of being hung on high has come upon me, like Manṣūr.

I am Manṣūr hanging from the branch of the gallows of the All-Merciful; such kissing and embracing has come upon me far from the lips of the vile ones."

Ho, kissing is done with; hide your heart like a turnover; within the breast utter secretly the words innumerable.

73

Today your beauty has another lineament, today your delectable lip has another sweetmeat;

Today your ruby rose has sprung from another twig, today your cypress-stature has another loftiness.

Today that moon of yours indeed is not contained in the sky, and that wheel-like die of yours has another expanse;

Today I know not from which side the commotion has arisen, I only know that through it the world has another riot.

5 That lion-overthrowing deer—it is evident in its eyes that outside the two worlds it has another desert.

This mad heart departed; both heart and madness became lost, for it has another madness loftier than this madness.

If he has no foot, the lover will fly on eternal wings, and if he has no head, the lover has other heads.

The sea of the two eyes sought him and became empty; it was not aware that another sea contains that pearl.

In love I turned the two worlds upside down; why did you seek him here? For he holds another place.

10   My heart's today is love, my heart's tomorrow the Beloved; my heart's today holds in its heart another tomorrow.

If King Ṣalāḥ al-Dīn is hidden, it is no wonder, for out of the jealousy of God every moment he has another master of the harem.

74

Morn-arising friends, who is there that discovers the dawn, who discovers us dancing in confusion like atoms?

Who has the luck to come to the brink of a river to drink water from that river, and to discover the reflection of the moon?

Who is there that like Jacob from the shirt of Joseph seeks the scent of his son, and instead discovers the light of his eyes?

Or athirst like the bedouin casts a bucket into the well, and in the bucket discovers a beauty like an ass-load of sugar?

5   Or like Moses seeking fire, who seeks out a bush, comes to gather the fire, and discovers a hundred dawns and sunrises?

Jesus leaps into the house to escape from the foe; suddenly from the house he discovers a passage to heaven.

Or like a Soloman he splits a fish, and in the belly of that fish he discovers a ring of gold.

Sword in hand, 'Umar comes intending to slay the Prophet; he falls into God's snare, and discovers a kindly regard from fortune.

Or like Adham's son he drives towards a deer to make the deer his prey, and instead discovers another prey.

10   Or like a thirsty oyster shell he comes with gaping mouth to take a drop of water into himself, and discovers a pearl within himself.

Or a man foraging who turns towards desolations, and suddenly in a desolation he discovers news of a treasure.

Traveller, have done with legends, so that intimate alike and stranger may discover without your exposition the light of *Did We not open.*

Whoever strides sincerely towards Shams al-Dīn, though his foot may grow weary, he will discover two wings from Love.

75

Friend, is sugar sweeter or He who makes the sugar? Friend, is the moon fairer or He who makes the moon?

Forgo sugars, forgo moons; He knows something other, He makes something other.

In the sea are marvels besides pearls, but none like the Monarch who makes the sea and the pearls.

Besides the water is another water springing from a marvellous waterwheel; without flaw and unsleeping It provides sustenance to the heart.

5   Without knowledge it is not possible to fashion an image of a bath; how shall be that Knowledge which makes intellect and awareness?

Without knowledge you cannot extract oil from fat; consider then that Knowledge which makes sight from fat.

Souls are distraught, without eating and slumber, on account of the marvellous feast which He makes at the time of dawn.

Happy dawn, when that despair of every moon makes His two hands a belt around my waist!

Yonder sky laughs at the mustachios of that deluded one; that laughingstock makes himself an ass in the train of two or three asses.

10   That ass flings himself into gold as if into barley; he is heedless of the King who makes gems of stones.

I have made enough, enough, I have quit exhalation; the rest that Darling will speak, who makes of the ear an eye.

76

That wandering slave has returned, returned; he has come before You burning and melting like a candle.

Smile upon him, O Soul, like anemone and sugar-candy; do not shut the door, O Soul, for he comes in need.

And even if You close the door, he will submit to Your decree; the servant is all servile need, the king is full of pride and disdain.

Every molten candle has become the brightness of the eye, for he who has suffered melting has become privy to the secret.

5   If I make a difference between envenomed water from His hand and wine, in the path of the Spirit my spirit has come, by Allah, but insincerely.

How should any animal drink His water of life? How should the eye which is closed behold His face?

I have abandoned travel, I have come to dwell with the Friend, I have become secure from death because that long life has come.

My heart, since you are in this stream why then do you still seek for water? How long will you say, "Come to the Feast"? The time of prayer has come.

77

Why must I dance in the glow of His sun? So that when the mote dances, He may remember me.

Every atom has become pregnant of the glow of His face, every atom of that delight gives birth to a hundred atoms.

Behold, in the mortar, how the body out of love for one fleet of spirit beats and bruises itself to become an atom.

If you are pearl and coral, only become grain-fine here, because in this presence only a mote is becoming.

5   Behold the pearl of the soul in the oyster shell of the body, how it bites its fingers at the hand of affliction.

When the spirit takes flight from you, this imprisoned essence returns to its origin like a mote—you may call to it, but it will not come.

And though its load be very firm and it digs in blood, though for a whole life it goes in blood, not one hair of it will be defiled.

Its only dwelling place is in the well of Babylon; until the soul becomes a magician, it reposes not in any place.

Tabriz! If Shams al-Dīn shines forth from your zodiac, even the cloud will become like the moon, even the moon will wax in brightness.

78

Every moment the Soul is decaying and growing before you, and how should any man plead with you for the sake of a single soul?

Wherever you set your foot a head springs from the earth; for one head's sake how should anyone wash his hands of you?

On the day when the soul takes flight in joy at your scent, the soul knows, the soul knows, what scent wafts from the Beloved.

Once your crop-sickness diminishes from the brain, the head raises a hundred laments, every hair is groaning.

5   I have emptied house, that I may be filled with your furniture; I am waning, that your love may wax and increase.

My soul in the train of Shams al-Ḥaqq-i Tabrīzī is scudding like a ship without feet over the sea.

79

Do not despair, my soul, for hope has manifested itself; the hope of every soul has arrived from the unseen.

Do not despair, though Mary has gone from your hands, for that light which drew Jesus to heaven has come.

Do not despair, my soul, in the darkness of this prison, for that king who redeemed Joseph from prison has come.

Jacob has come forth from the veil of occlusion, Joseph who rent Zulaikhā's veil has come.

5 You who all through night to dawn have been crying "O Lord," mercy has heard that "O Lord" and has come.

O pain which has grown old, rejoice, for the cure has come; O fastened lock, open, for the key has come.

You who have abstained fasting from the Table on high, break your fast with joy, for the first day of the feast has come.

Keep silence, keep silence, for by virtue of the command "Be!" that silence of bewilderment has augmented beyond all speech.

80

Die now, die now, in this Love die; when you have died in this Love, you will all receive new life.

Die now, die now, and do not fear this death, for you will come forth from this earth and seize the heavens.

Die now, die now, and break away from this carnal soul, for this carnal soul is as a chain and you are as prisoners.

Take an axe to dig through the prison; when you have broken the prison you will all be kings and princes.

5 Die now, die now before the beauteous King; when you have died before the King, you will all be kings and renowned.

Die now, die now, and come forth from this cloud; when you come forth from this cloud, you will all be radiant full moons.

Be silent, be silent; silence is the sign of death; it is because of life that you are fleeing from the silent one.

81

The weary ones have all gone; close the door of the house; laugh all in union at aweary reason.

Come forth to the Ascension, since you are of the Prophet's

family; kiss the cheek of the moon, since you are on a high roof.

Since he split the moon, why are you clouds? Since he is sprightly and neat, why are you good-for-nothing?

Weary ones, why did you depart? For not like true men on this path did you like Farhād and Shaddād in a moment cleave through the mountain.

5 Since you are not moon-faced, turn not away from the moon-faced; since you are not in anguish, do not bandage your own heads.

Like that it did happen and like this; so it comes not right; do not know how you are, do not know how many you are!

When you beheld that fountain, why did you not become water? When you saw that Self, why did you approve your own selves?

Since you are in the mine of sugarcane, why are you sour of face? Since you are in the Water of Life, why are you dry and withered?

Do not contend so, do not flee from felicity; what possibility of flight is there, seeing that you are in the toils of the lasso?

10 You are caught in the lasso from which there is no security; do not writhe, do not writhe, do not scrape against the shuttle.

Like self-sacrificing moths rub against this candle; why are you dedicated to the companion? Why are you attached to the chain?

Burn at this candle, light up your heart and soul, put on a new body when you have flung away this old one.

Why are you afraid of the fox? You are of lion stock. Why are you lame asses, since you are of the loins of the swift horse?

The Friend Himself is coming, the door of felicity is opening, for that friend is the key; you are all locks.

15 Be silent, for speech has swallowed you down; the purchaser is like a parrot, and you are all sugar-candy.

82

Since your image dwelt within the house of our breasts, wherever we sit has become like highest paradise.

Those thoughts and imaginings that were as Gog and Magog—each one has become like a houri's cheek and a doll of China.

That image on account of which men and women all weep, if it was once an evil companion, has now become an excellent companion.

Above all a garden has grown, below all is a treasure—what manner of thing are you, that through you the world has become so?

5   From that day when we beheld him we augment daily; the thorn that sought him out has become a veritable rosebower.

Every unripe grape has become a ripe grape from the sun and has become full of sugar, and that black stone too through the sun has become a precious ruby.

Many an earth there is that by God's preference has become a heaven, many a left hand through the palm of divine favour has become a right hand.

If once he was darkness to the heart, now he has become the heart's window; if once he was a footpad of the faith, now he has become the leader of religion.

If it was the well of calamity that was Joseph's prison, on account of his coming forth it became the firm cord.

10   Every particle like the army of God is subject to God's command; to the servant of God it has proved security, to the infidel it has become as an ambush.

Silence! For your speech is as the Nile—to the Copts like blood, to the Israelites a pure well.

Silence! For your speech is a ripe fig, only not every bird of the air is suitable for figs.

83

At the dawn hour a moon appeared in the sky, came down from the sky and gazed upon me.

Like a hawk which seizes a bird at the time of hunting, that moon snatched me up and ran over the sky.

When I gazed at myself I saw myself no more, because in that moon my body through grace became like the soul.

When I voyaged in soul I saw naught but the moon, so that
the secret of the eternal revelation was all disclosed.

5   The nine spheres of heaven were all absorbed in that moon,
the ship of my being was entirely hidden in the sea.

That sea surged, and Reason arose again and cast abroad a
voice; thus it happened and so it befell.

That sea foamed, and at every foam-fleck something took
form and something was bodied forth.

Every foam-fleck of body which received a sign from that
sea melted forthwith and became spirit in that sea.

Without the royal fortune of Shams al-Dīn of Tabriz one
could neither behold the moon nor become the sea.

84

Birds, who are now parted from your cage, show your faces
again and declare where you are.

Your ship has stopped on this water, wrecked; like fishes,
for one instant rise from this water.

Is it that the mould has broken and rejoined that Friend?
Or has the trap slipped out of hand, and you are parted from
the prey?

Are you today fuel to that fire of yourselves? Or has the fire
in you died, and are you the light of God?

5   Has that wind become a pestilence and congealed you? Or
has it become the breeze of the zephyr, wherever you enter?

There is an answer from your souls in every word that
proceeds, even though you may not open your mouths to
answer.

How many pearls you have broken in the mortar of the
days! That is surmeh to the eyes; pound on, pound on!

You who have been born when you arrived at death, this is
a second birth—be born, be born!

Whether you are born Hindu or Turk a second time will
become clear on the day when you remove the veil.

10   And if it be that you have been worthy of Shams al-Ḥaqq of
Tabriz, by Allah, you are the high chamberlains of the day of
retribution.

85

Though the whole world be full of thorns, the heart of the lover is wholly a rosebower;
And though heaven's wheel be idle and ineffective, the world of lovers is fully employed.
Let all other men be sorrowful, yet the lover's soul will be gay and happy and sprightly.
Give to the lover every place where a candle is extinguished, for he is endowed with a hundred thousand lights.
5 Even if the lover is alone, he is not alone, for his is companioned by the hidden Beloved.
The wine of lovers bubbles up from the breast; love's companion is in the inmost secrets.
Love is not content with a hundred promises, for the cunning of the heart-enchanters is manifold.
And if you should see a lover sick, is not the fair one at the sick one's head?
Be a rider of love, and fear not the way, for love's steed is swift of pace;
10 With a single bound it brings you to the abode, even though the road be not even.
The soul of the lover knows nothing of fodder-eating, for the souls of lovers are vintners of fine wine.
In Shams al-Dīn-i Tabrīzī you will discover a heart which is at once intoxicated and very sober.

86

Rajab has gone out and Sha'bān has entered; the soul has quit the body, and the Beloved has entered.
The breath of ignorance and the breath of heedlessness have gone forth; the breath of love and the breath of forgiveness have entered.
The heart is sprouting roses and eglantine and basil, since from the cloud of generosity rain has arrived.

The mouths of all the sorrowful ones are laughing because of this candy which has entered the teeth.

Man is wearing gold brocade like the sun, since that gold-scattering moon-faced one has entered.

Clap hands and speak, minstrel of love, for that ringleader of trouble has entered stamping feet.

If yesterday has gone, may today remain forever, and if 'Umar has departed, 'Uthmān has entered.

All the past life is returning, since this eternal prosperity has entered.

If you are drunk and asleep in the ship of Noah, why should you worry if the Flood has arrived?

o The earth of Tabriz has become lit up like the sky, since Shams al-Dīn has entered that maidan.

87

We have departed—may the remainder long remain! Inescapably every man who has been born must depart.

Heaven's bowl has never seen any dish that did not in the end fall from the roof.

Do not run about so, for in this earth the pupil has become even as the master.

Lovely one, put not on airs, for in this grave many a Shīrīn has become naughted, the same as Farhād.

5 After all, what constancy is there in an edifice whose columns are but fragments of wind?

If we were evil, we carried away evil; if we were good, then may you remember!

Though you may be the unique one of your time, today you will be departing as one by one.

If you do not wish to remain alone, make children of obedience to God and good actions.

That thread of unseen light is immortal, because it is the pith of the spirit of the Pegs;

o That essence of love, which is the quintessence—that remains to all eternity.

If these shifting sands are unstable, another kind of foundation is laid down.

I am like Noah's ark in this dry land, for that flood is the sealing of the promised time.

Noah made his house an ark, because he saw from the unseen the wave overtowering.

We have fallen asleep amongst the silent ones, because we have passed all bounds in clamour and lamentation.

88

That Joseph handsome of cheek has come, that Jesus of the age has come;

That banner of a hundred thousand victories has come fluttering over the cavalcade of spring.

You whose business it is to bring the dead to life, arise, for the day of work has come.

The lion which seizes lions a-hunting has come into the meadowland raging drunk.

5   Yesterday and the day before have departed; seize the cash, for that coin of fair assay has come.

This city today is like paradise; it is saying, "The Prince has come."

Beat the drum, for it is the day of festival; be joyous, for the Friend has come.

A moon has lifted its head out of the unseen, in comparison with which this moon has become as dust;

Because of the beauty of that souls' repose, the whole world has become restless.

10   Take heed, spread open the skirt of love, for sprinkling has come from the ninth heaven.

O exile bird with cut pinions, in the place of two wings four have come.

Ho, heart bound in breast, open, for that lost one has come into your bosom.

Foot, come and stamp foot, for that illustrious cupbearer has come.

Speak not of the old man, for he has become young, and speak not of yesteryear, for the Friend has come.

15   You said, "What excuse shall I utter to the king?" The king himself has come making excuses.

You said, "Whither shall I escape out of his hand?" His hand has come bringing all succour.

You saw a fire, and light has come; you saw blood, and red wine has come.

That one who was fleeing from his own fortune, having fled, has come back shamefaced.

Be silent, and count not his graces; an innumerable grace it is that has come.

89

We have become drunk and our heart has departed, it has fled from us—whither has it gone?

When it saw that the chain of reason was broken, immediately my heart took to flight.

It will not have gone to any other place, it has departed to the seclusion of God.

Seek it not in the house, for it is of the air; it is a bird of the air, and has gone into the air.

5   It is the white falcon of the Emperor; it has taken flight, and departed to the Emperor.

90

We are foes to ourselves, and friends to him who slays us; we are drowned in the sea, and the waves of the sea are slaying us.

For this reason, laughing and gay, we are yielding up sweet life, because that king is slaying us with honey and sugar and sweetmeat.

We make ourselves out fat for the sacrifice of the feast, because that butcher of lovers slays the very fine and handsome.

That Iblis without light begs for a respite from Him; He gave him respite, because He is slaying him after tomorrow.

5   Like Ishmael, cheerfully lay your neck before the knife; do
not steal your throat away from Him, if He is slaying, until
He slays.

Azrael has no power or way to overcome lovers; love itself
and passion slays the lovers of love.

The slain ones shout, "Would that my people knew"; se-
cretly the Beloved bestows a hundred lives, and openly slays.

Put forth a head out of the earth of the body, and then see
that He is either drawing you to heaven, or slaying you.

The spirit of breath He takes away, the comfort spiritual
He bestows; He releases the falcon of the soul, and slays the
owl of sorrow.

10   That idea the Christian carries abroad, the Moslem has not
that idea, that He is slaying this Messiah upon the cross.

Every true lover is like Manṣūr, they slay themselves; show
any beside the lover who deliberately slays himself!

Death daily makes a hundred requisitions on mankind; the
lover of God without requisition slays himself.

I make this enough, else I will myself utter the lovers'
secret, though the unbeliever slays himself of anger and fury.

Shams-i Tabrīzī has climbed over the horizon like the sun;
unceremoniously he is extinguishing the candles of the stars.

91

Behold, those birds which lay golden eggs every morning
saddle the swift colt of the skies.

When they gallop, the seventh heaven is their arena; when
they sleep, they are a pillow for the sun and the moon.

They are fishes, in the soul of each one of which is a Jonah;
they are rosebushes which beautify and order well the skies.

Hell-tasters, heaven-givers, on the day of resurrection they
are the rulers, they know neither any blessing nor utter any
imprecation.

5   They set the mountains dancing of subtlety in the air, and
convert the seas in sweetness to be like sweet sugar.

They make bodies souls, and souls everlasting; they make
stones into ruby mines, and unbelief into faith.

They are more manifest than all, and more hidden than all; if you wish to behold them, they make themselves visible before your eyes.

If you wish to behold clearly, make surmeh of the dust of their feet; for they cause him who was blind from his mother's womb to see the way.

If you are a thorn, be sharp of point as a thorn in the quest, that they may convert your whole thorn into the likeness of roses and eglantine.

If there were scope for speech, I would utter things that may be spoken, so that the spirits and the angels applauded out of heaven.

92

Last night our elephant remembered India again, in frenzy he was rending the veil of night till dawn.

Last night the flagons of the sakis were all overbrimming — O may our life be like last night till the day of resurrection!

The wines were bubbling and the reasons were senseless on account of him; may part and whole, thorn and rose be happy because of his lovely face!

The cup-on-cup clamour of the drunkards mounted to heaven; in our hands was the wine, and in our heads the wind.

Thousands of uproars fell upon the skies because of these, there hundreds of thousands of Kai-Qubāds were fallen prostrate.

The day of triumph and good fortune was contained in our night; of the brethren of purity night suddenly gave birth to such a day.

The sea broke into waves; heaven received a token of this night, and in pride set that token on its head and face.

Whatever ways humanity had closed in darkness, the light of divinity in compassion was opening up.

How should the sensible forms on account of that passion remain in place? How should he remain in place who attains this desire?

Begin life anew, Moslems! For the Beloved has converted non-entity into being, and dispensed justice to the lovers.

Our Beloved henceforward holds the fallen to be pardon-able, because wherever He is the saki no one remains on the right course.

The surging of the sea of grace, Moslems, has wrecked the pomp of personal effort and the programme of belief.

That grace is King Ṣalāḥ al-Dīn, for he is a Joseph whom the Lord of Egypt himself must purchase at a great price.

93

I have come to lay my face in the dust of the Beloved's feet, I have come to beg pardon for a moment for my actions.

I have come to take up anew the service of His rosebower, I have come to bring fire and set my thorns alight.

I have come to get purification from the dust of all that has passed, to reckon my good deeds as evil as performed in the cause of my Beloved;

I have come with eyes weeping, that my eyes may behold paradise—fountains consisting of the love of that blandisher of mine.

5   Rise, disencumbered passion, take up love anew; I have died and become void of my old faith and unbelief;

For without your straining-cloth it is impossible to become unsullied in existence, without You it is impossible ever to escape from one's sorrows and griefs.

Outwardly I have fallen silent; but You know that in-wardly I have bloodstained speech in my blood-consuming heart.

In this state of silence examine well my face, that You may see on my cheeks a myriad traces of yourself.

I have shortened this ode; the rest of it is in my heart; I will utter it, if You intoxicate me with your vintner eye.

10   O silent from speaking, O you sundered from your mate, how did you become thus distraught from your clever reason?

Silent one, how are you faring with these fiery thoughts? Thoughts are arriving with their huge-panoplied army.

When people are alone, they are silent; one speaks with men, no one speaks the secret of his heart to door and wall.

Perchance you find no men to talk with, that you have fallen silent? Perchance you see no man to be intimate with your words?

Are you haply of the pure world? Do not you mix with material things, with dogs of natural being who are defiled with their own carrion?

94

The dead would rend his shroud and rise from the tomb, if that dead man had tidings of my Idol.

What will dead and living do when he discovers something of Him? For if the mountain beheld Him, it would leap and advance.

I will not flee from blame, for the blame comes from you; from your bitterness all the taste of sugar comes to the soul.

Devour whatever has come to you, leave it not to store up, for you are on the banks of a running stream—when you have drunk, more will come.

Behold His fair handiwork, listen to His inspiration to the hearts; become entirely light of vision—all rapture comes from vision.

Do not despair, saying, "My life is gone, and the Friend has not come"; He comes betimes and out of season, He comes not only at dawn.

Be watchful and wakeful in season and out of season, for suddenly our King enters the eyes like 'Uzaizī antimony.

When He enters this eye, this eye becomes like the sea; when He gazes on the sea, out of all its waters pearls come;

Not such a dead pearl that knows not its own essence, pearls will come all speaking, all seeking, altogether alive.

What do you know, what do you know what kind of mind and soul you are? It is God who knows and sees the virtue that belongs to men.

Become accustomed to speak without lips, like a balance, for lips and teeth do not remain when one passes from the world.

95

Say, do not despair because the Beloved drives you away; if He drives you away today, will He not call you back tomorrow?

If He shuts the door on you, do not go away; be patient there, for after patience He will seat you in the place of honour.

And if He bars against you all ways and passages, He will show you a secret way, which no man knows.

Is it not the case that when the butcher cuts off the head of a sheep with his knife, he does not abandon what he has slain, but first slays, and then draws?

5 When no more breath remains to the sheep, he fills it with his own breath; you will see whither God's breath will bring you!

I spoke this as a parable; else, His generosity slays no man, rather it rescues him from slaying.

He gives all the kingdom of Solomon to a single ant; He bestows both worlds, and does not startle a single heart.

My heart has travelled round the world and found none like Him; whom does He resemble? Whom does He resemble?

Ah, silence! For without speech He gives to all of this wine to taste, He gives to taste, He gives to taste, He gives to taste.

96

Ho, lovers, labour so that, when body and soul remain no more, your hearts may fly to heaven, not remain heavy like the body.

Wash your hearts and souls in the water of wisdom clean of dust, ho, that the two eyes of regret may not remain turned towards the earth.

Is it not the case with everything in the world, that love is its vital soul? Apart from love, everything you see remains not eternally.

Your nonexistence (before birth) is as the east, your death is as the west, oriented to another heaven that resembles not this visible heaven.

The way to heaven is within; shake the wings of love— when love's wings have become strong, there is no need to trouble about a ladder.

Consider not the world that exists without, for the true world is within the eye; when you have shut your eyes on the world, the world will not remain.

Your heart is like a roof, and your senses are waterspouts; drink water from the roof, for the waterspout remains not for ever.

Recite entirely this ode from the tablet of the heart; regard not the tongue, for lips and tongue do not remain.

Man's body is a bow, breath and speech are as its arrows; once the arrows and quiver have gone, no more work remains for the bow.

97

All slept, and yet sleep did not transport me, heart-forlorn as I am; all night my eyes counted the stars in the sky.

Sleep had so departed from my eyes as if never to return; my sleep had quaffed the poison of separation from you, and expired.

How would it be if you concocted a remedy out of encounter for one wounded, who has committed his heart and eyes to your hands?

No, it is not right to close the door of beneficence once and for all; if you will not give pure wine, less than one mouthful of dregs will you not give?

God has placed all manners of delight in a single chamber; no man without you ever found the right way into that chamber.

If I have become dust in the path of love, regard me not as insignificant; how should he who beats on the door of union with you be insignificant?

Fill my sleeve with unseen pearls—a sleeve which has wiped many a tear from these eyes.

Whenever the policeman of love has constrained anyone on a dark night, your moon has compassionately pressed him in its silvery bosom.

If the wandering heart returns of your grace, it is the story of the night, the disk of the moon, the camel, and the Kurd.

10 Were not these inanimates originally of water? The world is a cold place; it came and congealed one by one.

Our blood in our body is the water of life, and sweet; when it comes forth from its place, see how it is all the same!

Do not congeal the water of speech, and bring it not from that fountain, so that it is silk on that side and striped cloth on this.

98

Have you heard that sugar has become cheap in the town? Have you heard that winter has vanished and summer is here?

Have you heard that basil and carnation in the garden are laughing surreptitiously because affairs have become easy?

Have you heard that the nightingale has returned from his travels, joined in the concert and become the master of all the birds?

Have you heard that now in the garden the branches of the trees have heard glad news of the rose, and shake their hands?

5 Have you heard that the soul has become drunk from the cup of spring, and gone off gay and dancing into the Sultan's sanctuary?

Have you heard that the anemone's cheeks are suffused with blood? Have you heard that the rose has become head chamberlain of the divan?

Have you heard about the thievishness of mad December, how the just officer of spring has come, and he has disappeared?

These idols have obtained laissez-passer from the divan, so that the earth has become green and arrayed in full splendour.

If the beauties of the garden last year wrought wonders, each one this year has emerged in beauty a hundredfold as great.

10 Rose-cheeked ones have come forth whirling out of nonexist-

ence, such that the stars in heaven are but scatter before their feet.

The deposed narcissus has become the inspector of the kingdom; the infant bud like Jesus has become understanding and chanting.

The feast of these creatures of joy has once more taken on ornament; once more the breeze of the zephyr bestows wine on the garden.

There were images hidden behind the veil of the heart; the orchards have become mirrors to the secret of their hearts.

Whatever you behold, seek from the heart, do not seek from the mirror; the mirror may receive an image, but it cannot become alive.

15 All the dead ones of the garden have come to life at the summons of God; their unbelief by God's mercy has all been turned to faith.

They are continuing in their shrouds, and are all stirring, for that which is alive cannot become pledged for ever to prison;

He said, "Make this enough, for I will expound this better than this." I shut my mouth, for He had come and become surety.

The King's lips will likewise describe all completely, if the summary has departed from you into the bosom of concealment.

99

This fledgling pigeon essayed the air and flew off when he heard a whistle and a call from the unseen.

When that Desire of all the world sent a messenger saying, "Come to Me," how should not the disciple's soul take flight?

How should it not fly upwards on discovering such pinions, how should it not rend the body's robe on the arrival of such a missive?

What a moon it is that draws all these souls! What a way is that secret way by which it drew!

5 Divine compassion sent a letter saying, "Come back hither, for in this narrow cage your soul has fluttered much.

But in the house without doors you are like a bird without wings; so the fowl of the air does when it has fallen low.

Restlessness opens to it the door of compassion at last; beat your wings against door and roof—this is the key.

Until you call on Me, you do not know the way of returning; for by Our calling the way becomes manifest to the reason."

Whatever mounts up, if it be old it becomes new; whatever new descends here, through time it becomes threadbare.

10   Ho, strut proudly into the unseen, do not look back, in God's protection, for there all is profit and increase.

Ha, silent one, depart to the Saki of Being, who gave you His pure wine in this sullied cup.

100

Lord, is this sweet scent coming from the meadow of the soul, or is it a breeze wafting from beyond the world?

Lord, from what homeland does this water of life bubble up? Lord, from what place comes this light of the attributes?

Amazing! Does this clamour arise from the troop of the angels? Amazing! Does this laughter come from the houris of paradise?

What concert is it, that the soul spins round dancing? What whistle is it, that the heart is coming flapping wings?

5   What a marriage feast it is! What a wedding! Heaven is like a curtain; the moon with this plate of gold for a sign is coming.

What a hunt! For the arrow of fate is flying; if it is not so, why comes the sound of the bow?

Good news, good news, lovers all! Clap your hands, for he who once escaped from your hands is coming clapping.

From the fortress of the skies the cry of "safe quarter" is arising, and from the sea such a wave of fear is coming.

The eye of prosperity is intoxicated with your approaching; this is a proof that is obvious to the eye.

10   Escape from this world of dearth, where lances strike for the sake of two or three loaves.

What is fairer than life? Yet if life should go, have no fear; why do you grieve about its departing, seeing that better than it is coming?

Every man is amazed at something; my amazement is, how it

is that when He enters the midst, He is not contained in the
midst.
Let me have done. Though it is a cipher, I will not explain it;
what are you trying to explain? The soul of explanation is
coming.

101

Amazing keeper of the hot baths! When he comes forth from
seclusion, every painted figure of the baths falls into prostration!
The figures, frozen, unconscious, dead—from the reflection of
his eyes their eyes open large as narcissi.
Through his ears their ears become familiar with fables,
through his eyes their eyes become receptive of vistas.
You behold every single bath-figure drunk and dancing, like a
boon companion who from time to time plunges in red wine.
The courtyard of the baths is full of their clamour and shout-
ing; the riotous clamour marks the first day of resurrection.
The figures call one another unto themselves; one figure from
that corner there comes laughing to another figure.
But no form discovers the bath-keeper himself, for all that
form is running hither and thither in search of him.
All are distracted, he behind and before them, unrecognized,
the king of the souls comes at the head of the army.
The rosebed of every mind is filled with roses from his cheeks;
the skirt of every beggar is filled with gold from his hand.
Hold your basket before him, that he may fill it of himself, so
that the basket of your poverty may become the despair of
Sanjar.
Judge and plaintiff alike flee from less and more, when that
moon for one moment enters drunk into the assembly.
The wine becomes the tavern, the dead become riotous drunk,
the wood becomes the Moaning Pillar when he enters the pulpit.
He denies them his presence, and their forms freeze, their eyes
vanish, their ears become deaf.
When he appears again their eyes open, the garden becomes
full of birds, the orchard is verdant.
Go to the rosebed and the garden, behold the friends and the

chatter; in the wake of this expression the soul comes to that pass.

How can one tell what was manifested, friend? How can the pen indite that, for all that it enters the inkholder?

102

Little by little the drunkards congregate, little by little the wine-worshippers arrive.

The heart-cherishers coquettishly come along the way, the rosy-cheeked ones are arriving from the garden.

Little by little from the world of being and not-being the not-beings have departed and the beings are arriving.

All with skirts full of gold as a mine are arriving for the sake of the destitute.

5   The lean and sick from the pasturage of love are arriving fat and hale.

The souls of the pure ones like the rays of the sun are arriving from such a height to the lowly ones.

Blessed is that garden, where, for the sake of the Mary's, new fruits are arriving even in winter.

Their origin is grace, and their return is grace; even from the garden to the garden they are coming.

103

Laughter tells of your lovingkindness, tears complain of your wrath;

These two mutually contrary messages relate in this world about a single Beloved.

Lovingkindness beguiles a heedless man in such a way that he is not anxious about wrath, and commits sin;

The other man wrath endows with hopelessness, so that he keeps complete despair.

Love, like a pitying intercessor, comes to the protection of both these lost souls.

We give thanks for this love, O God, which performs infinite lovingkindnesses;

Whatever shortcomings in our gratitude we may be guilty of, love suffices to make amends for it.

Is this love Kauthar, or the Water of Life? It makes life without bound and term;

Between the sinner and God, like the Messenger, it runs much to and fro and busies itself greatly.

o   Make an end of verse on verse; do not recite this; love itself will interpret the verse.

104

The lovers visible and the Beloved invisible—who ever saw such a love in all the world?

Not one lip having attained the form of the Beloved, hundreds of thousands of souls have expired.

Two bowshots' distance shot an arrow from the heights, so that it tore through the shields of the skies.

Not having drawn the skirt of the Beloved of the Unseen, the hearts of thousands have suffered tribulation and beating;

Not having bitten the lip of Him whose lip is sweet, how many have bitten the back of the hand in banishment!

Not having grazed on the sugar-cane of His lip, the heart has grazed on His thousands of blandishments.

Not one rose having blossomed from His rosegarden, hundreds of thousands of thorns have pricked in the breast.

Though the soul has experienced nothing but cruelty from Him, it has fled away from mortal fidelities in hope of Him;

It has preferred that pain over generosities, and has chosen that cruelty above all fidelities.

o   His thorn has triumphed over all roses, His lock is more delightful than a hundred keys.

His tyranny has carried off the ball from the turn of good fortune; candies have blossomed from the poison of His wrath.

His rejection is better than the reception of others; ruby and pearl are desirous of His stone.

These worldly happinesses are nothing; seek that happiness which Bū Saʿīd possesses.

These augmentations of this world are less; seek that augmentation which Bā Yazīd possesses.

15 That augmentation is your six-fingered hand; its value is less, though apparently it is augmenting.

Seek that radiance which Sanāʾī expounded, that Unique One whose uniqueness ʿAṭṭār revealed.

Fat and sweet food appear pure and good; one night they passed with you, and became filth.

Eat the fat and sweet of the food of love, that your wings may sprout and you may know how to fly.

After all, Abraham as a child in the cave sucked from the fingertips of a lion.

20 Dismiss that; that foetus in the womb sucked the water of life from blood.

The tall stature which heaven made upright in the end became bowed like the crooked heaven;

The tall stature which Love raised up, its stature transcended the glorious Throne.

Nay, be silent; He who knows all secrets is present; He said, *We are nearer than the jugular vein.*

105

Our death is an eternal wedding-feast; what is the secret of this? *He is God, One.*

The sun became dispersed through the windows; the windows became shut, and the numbers departed.

Those numbers which existed in the grapes are naughted in the juice which flows from the grapes.

Whosoever is living by the light of God, the death of this spirit is replenishment to him.

5 Speak not evil, speak not good regarding those who have passed away from good and evil.

Fix your eye on God, and speak not of what you have not seen, that He may implant another eye in your eye.

That eye is the eye of the eye, nothing unseen or secret escapes from it.

When its gaze is by the Light of God, to such a light what can be hidden?

Though all lights are the Light of God, call not all of those the eternal Light.

10 Eternal light is that which is the Light of God, transient light is the attribute of flesh and body.

The light in this mortal eye is a fire, save for that eye which God anoints with surmeh.

His fire became light for the sake of Abraham; the eye of reason became in quality like the eye of an ass.

O God, the bird of the eye which has seen Your bounty flies in Your air.

The Pole, he who is the sky of the skies, is on the lookout in search of You;

15 Either grant him vision to see You, or do not dismiss him on account of this fault.

Make tearful the eye of your soul every moment, guard it against the snare of human stature and cheek.

Eye asleep and yourself wakeful—such a sleep is perfection and rectitude;

But the eye asleep that finds no interpretation (of dreams)— expel it from sleep, despite envy.

Else it will labour and be boiling in the fire of love of the One, even to the grave.

106

Everywhere the secret of God is coming—see how the people are coming uncontrollably;

From him for whom all souls are athirst, to the thirsty the cry of the water carrier is coming.

They are milk drinkers of divine generosity, and are on the watch to see from whence the mother is coming.

They are in separation, and all are waiting to see whence union and encounter are coming.

5   From Moslems, Jews, and Christians alike every dawn the sound of prayer is coming;

Blessed is that intelligence into whose heart's ear from heaven the sound of "Come hither" is coming.

Keep your ear clean of scum, for a voice is coming from heaven;

The defiled ear hears not that sound—only the deserving gets his deserts.

Defile not your eye with human cheek and mole, for that Emperor of eternal life is coming;

10   And if it has become defiled, wash it with tears, for the cure comes from those tears.

A caravan of sugar has arrived from Egypt; the sound of footfall and bells is coming.

Ha, be silent, for to complete the ode our speaking King is coming.

107

Again the sun of felicity has mounted to heaven, again the desire of the souls has arrived from the way of the soul.

Again by the good pleasure of Riḍwān the gates of paradise have been opened, every spirit is plunged up to its neck in the pool of Kauthar.

Again that King, who is the altar to whom kings turn, has entered, again that Moon surpassing the moon has entered.

These distraught by mad passion have all mounted their steeds, for that King, the unique cavalier, has entered the heart of the army.

5   The particles of dark earth are all bewildered and amazed, having heard from placelessness the cry, "Arise, the resurrection has come!"

The inexpressible proclamation has come, not from within and not from without, not left, not right, not behind, not from before.

You say, "What direction is that?" That direction where there is questing. You say, "Whither shall I turn my face?" Thither this head has come;

Thither whence this ripeness came upon the fruits, thither
whence the attributes of gems came upon the stones;
Thither where the dry fish came to life before Khiḍar, thither
whence Moses' hand became as a radiant moon.
10 This burning in our hearts has become bright as a candle, this
decree has come upon our heads like a crown of pride.
The soul has not leave to utter this exposition, else every
infidel would have escaped from unbelief.
The unbeliever in hardship turns his face thither; when he
experiences pain on this side, he believes in that side.
Continue in pain, that pain may show you the road thither;
that place who sees? The man who is constrained by pain.
That most mighty Emperor has closed the door fast; today he
has put on human apparel and entered by the door.

108

The sea can always dispense with the fish, for in comparison
with the sea the fish is contemptible.
You will not find fish, my soul, like the sea of the ocean; in the
sea of God's ocean there are many fish.
The sea is like a nurse, the fish like a sucking child; the
wretched infant is always weeping for milk.
Yet for all this indifference, if the sea should compassionately
incline towards a fish, great will be the grace;
5 And that fish which knows that the sea is seeking him—his
foot in pride rises above the ether.
That fish which—the sea does no task without the fish's opin-
ion is its counsellor—
You might say that so highly favoured a fish is an emperor,
and that infinite sea is his minister.
If anyone should dare to call him a fish, every drop in his
wrath would be as an arrow.
How long will you speak in riddles? Your riddles bring bewil-
derment; expound a little more clearly, that the heart may
perceive.
10 Worshipful Shams-i Dīn is both Lord and Master, for by him
the earth of Tabriz is all musk and ambergris.

Should the thorns of the world behold his graces, in softness and delicacy they would become like silk.

May I never have a soul, if my soul after tasting his wine and being drunk with his beauty is self-aware.

109

There was no grace left which that fair idol did not perform; what fault is it of ours, if he acted not generously towards you?

You are upbraiding because that beauty was cruel; whoever saw a lovely one in both worlds who acted not cruelly?

His love is sugar enough, even if he gave not sugar; his beauty is all fidelity, even if he was not faithful.

Show me a house that is not filled with lamps of him; show me a portico which his cheek has not filled with brightness.

5   This eye and that lamp are two lights, each one on its own; when the two met, none made parting between them.

When the spirit became lost in contemplation, it said this: "None has contemplated the beauty of God but God."

Each one of these similitudes is at once an exposition and an error; only out of jealousy God named His Face, *By the Forenoon*.

The sun of the face of Shams al-Dīn, Pride of Tabriz, never shone on aught transient but it made it eternal.

110

The fire the day before yesterday whispered secretly to the smoke, "The aloes-wood cannot rest without me, and with me it is happy.

It knows well my worth, and expresses thanks to me, for the aloes-wood has perceived that in its passing away there is profit.

The aloes-wood was knotted and tied from head to foot; in the release of nonexistence these knots were resolved.

Hail and welcome to you, my flame-eating friend, my passer-away and martyr and pride of all witnesses."

5   See how heaven and earth are pawns of existence; flee into nonexistence from the blindness of the one and the blueness of the other.

Every soul which flees away from poverty and nonexistence is misfortune fleeing away from prosperity and good fortune.

Without expunging, no one profits from the tablet of nonexistence; make peace between me and expunging, O loving One!

Until yonder dark earth passed away from itself, it did not begin to augment or escape from inertia.

So long as sperm was sperm and did not become obliterated from seminal fluid, it attained not the cypress' stature nor the cheeks' beauty.

10   When bread and broth ferment in the intestines, they then become reason and soul, the despair of the envious.

So long as black rock did not pass away from itself, it did not become gold and silver, neither found its way into coins.

First comes lowliness and bondage, then afterwards there is kingship; in the ritual prayer men first stand, and then sit.

For a lifetime you have made trial of your own being; once it is also necessary to experience not-being.

The pomp and pride of poverty and passing-away is no empty boast; whenever smoke appears, it is not without a fire.

15   If our minds and desires belong not to love, how did love wantonly rob us of heart and turban?

Love entered, and draws us along by the ear every morning to the school of *those who fulfil their covenants.*

Love sets flowing the water of penitence from the eye of the believer, to wash his breast clean of anger and stubborn denial.

You are fallen asleep and the water of Khiḍar splashes beside you; leap up from slumber and seize the goblet of immortality.

Let love tell you the rest of it secretly from me; be one with the Companions of the Cave, alike *sleeping* and *waking.*

III

The sweetheart appeared asleep. I called from the garden, "Quick, I have stolen a peach!" The sweetheart in fact was not asleep;

He laughed and said, "The fox then with cunning—how did it so easily steal the quarry from the lion's hands?"

Who milks a cloud? Who succeeds in reaching there, unless perchance the cloud of itself shows generosity?

How can the nonexistent contrive to bring into existence? It is God's bounty that bestows existence on the nonexistent.

5   Sit as if nonexistent; for in ritual prayer one only gives the greeting when seated.

It is through humility that water avails against fire, for fire stands up whereas water is prostrate.

When the lip is silent, the heart has a hundred tongues; be silent—how long, how long do you desire to make trial of Him?

I I 2

Dawn has arrived and drawn his polished blade, and from heaven camphor-white morn has broken forth.

The Sufi of the skies has rent his blue robe and shawl deliberately even to the navel.

After being routed, the Rumi of day having found the strength has dragged the Zangi of night from the royal throne.

From that direction whence the Turk of joy and the Hindu of grief arrived there is everlasting going and coming, and the way is not to be seen.

5   O Lord, whither has the army of the Abyssinian king fled? Whence so suddenly has the army of the Caesar of Rum arrived?

Who can catch the scent of this invisible road wrapped in enigma? He who has drunk or tasted of the wine of love pre-eternal.

Night is bewildered at who has blackened its face; day is bewildered at who has created it so fair.

Earth is bewildered at how one half of it became grass, and the other half grazing, and grazed upon that continually;

Half of it became eater and half for eating, half eager for purity and the other half impure.

10   Night has died and come to life again; it is life after death. O sorrow, slay me, for I am Ḥusain and you are Yazīd.

The pearl held auction, saying, "Who will buy this?" None had the price, so the pearl bought itself from itself.

Saki, today we have all become your guests; every night through you has become a Night of Power, every day a day of festival.

Give from your bowl the wine of *they shall be given to drink of pure wine,* for only new joy will cut away anxiety.

The heart-thirsty reprobates, when they drink wine to excess, when they lose themselves, then they find that key.

15 You have taken up your station beside the vat of Unity along with Noah and Lot and Karkhī and Shiblī and Bā Yazīd.

Be silent; for the spirit in joy is flapping its wings, so that that draught has coursed into the head and veins of the spirit.

113

Unbelief has put on black garments; the Light of Muhammad has arrived. The drum of immortality has been beaten; the eternal kingdom has arrived.

The face of earth is turned green; heaven has rent her robe; once again the moon is split; the incorporeal spirit has arrived.

The world is filled with sugar; happiness has bound its waist; arise, for once again that moon-cheeked one has arrived.

The heart like an astrolabe has become the token of the seven heavens; the commentary on the heart of Ahmad has arrived in seven volumes.

5 One night shackled reason approached the sultan of love, saying, "Fettered spirit has arrived to your good favour."

The messenger of the lovers' hearts ran head-downwards like a pen; the good tidings sweet as sugar have arrived in the heart of the page.

How long will the pure spirits endure under the earth? Ho, leap forth from the tomb—God-assisted victory has arrived.

The drum of resurrection has been beaten, the trumpet of uprising is sounding; the time has come, you dead ones—the mustering renewed has arrived.

Scattered is what is in the tombs, known is what is in the breasts; the voice of the trumpet has sounded; the spirit has arrived at its goal.

10 Last night a tumult arose amongst the stars, for the most auspicious star arrived from the propitious ones.

Mercury became out of control, he broke the Tablet and the Pen; in his wake Venus leaped, drunken arrived at the Pole Star. The moon's orb grew pale, she fled towards Leo. I said, "I trust all is well"; she said, "The unselfed saki has arrived."

Reason in the midst of that tumult desired to show itself; a child is still a child, even if it has arrived at the ABC.

Arise, for this is our turn, the King of the world is ours; since His gaze fell upon our souls, eternal life has arrived.

15 The saki without hue and bragging has poured out wine unstinted; the mountain of Qāf danced like a camel; joy extended has arrived.

The Solomon of the spirit has again cried, "Welcome to the morning cup!" The pavilion smoothed has arrived to dazzle Bilqīs.

Despite the envious ones of religion, in defiance of the accursed devil, the salve of heart and eye has arrived in the ophthalmic eye.

For the sake of the uninitiated I have clapped a lock on my mouth; minstrel, arise and cry, "Eternal delight has arrived."

I I 4

A little fox carried off the sheep's tail; was the lion perchance asleep? The blind and blue fox does not carry off its own life from the lion.

The lion purposely gave way, otherwise who would believe this, that the lame fox stole the sheep's tail from the lion?

He says, "A wolf ate Joseph son of Jacob"; even the lion of the skies cannot loose its talons on him.

Every moment the inspiration of God is guarding our hearts; how should the envious devil snatch our felicity from us?

5 God's hand is outstretched; do not seek to cheat God's hand; whoever sows a grain in God's path reaps barleycorn by barleycorn.

Whoever humiliates you, go, commit him to God; whoever seeks to dismay you, quickly turn your face to God.

Agony and fear and suffering are God's lasso; pain brings you pulling at your ear to the portal of bounty.

"Lord, Lord!" exclaiming, face to heaven turning, tears from your eyes running over your pale cheeks like a river—
     Green herbage sprung from the water over your desolate heart and soul, dawn stripping off the veil—*That is the Day of Eternity.*
10   If Pharaoh's head had ached with pain and tribulation, how would that rebel have uttered the boast of divinity?
     When the moment of drowning arrived he cried, "I am the least of slaves"; unbelief became faith, and he saw, when calamity showed its face.
     Withhold not suffering from your body; plunge it into the current of the Nile, so that your Pharaoh-like body may be purified of stubborn denial.
     The carnal soul is prince in Egypt, it is a prisoner in the current of the Nile; be like Gabriel over it, bring smoke out of the aloes-wood.
     It is a miserly aloes-wood, it will not convey scent to you nor unlock its secret until it endures fire and smoke.
15   The Pride of Tabriz, Shams-i Ḥaqq u Dīn whispered, "Love is sour-faced with you: it is not fitting to add more vinegar."

115

     The month of fasting has come, the emperor's banner has arrived; withhold your hand from food, the spirit's table has arrived.
     The soul has escaped from separation and bound nature's hands; the heart of error is defeated, the army of faith has arrived.
     The army of *the snorting chargers* has put its hand to plunder, from the fire of *the strikers of fire* the soul is brought to lamentation.
     The *Cow* was goodly, Moses son of 'Imrān appeared; through him the dead became living when it was sacrificed.
5   Fasting is as our sacrifice, it is the life of our soul; let us sacrifice all our body, since the soul has arrived as guest.
     Fortitude is as a sweet cloud, wisdom rains from it, because it was in such a month of fortitude that the Koran arrived.

When the carnal soul is in need, the spirit goes into Ascension; when the gate of the prison is broken, the soul reaches the Beloved.

The heart has rent the curtain of darkness and winged up to the sky; the heart, being of the angels, has again arrived at them.

Quickly clutch the rope out of this body's well; at the top of the well of water cry, "Joseph of Canaan has arrived."

10   When Jesus escaped from the ass his prayers became accepted; wash your hands, for the Table has arrived from heaven.

Wash your hands and your mouth, neither eat nor speak; seek that speech and that morsel which has come to the silent ones.

116

Hold on the skirt of His grace, for suddenly He will flee; but do not draw Him as an arrow, for He will flee from the bow.

What images does He play at, what tricks contrive! If He is present in form, He will flee by the way of spirit.

Seek Him in the sky, and He shines from the water like the moon; enter the water, and He flees up to heaven.

Call Him from the placeless and He points you to place; seek Him in place and He flees to the placeless.

5   Is not the bird of your imagination fleet as an arrow in existence? Know that for a certainty the Absolute flees from the imaginary.

I will flee from this and that out of fear (not out of weariness) because my gracious Beauty flees from this and that.

Fleet of foot as the wind am I for love of the Rose, not the rose that for fear of the autumn wind flees from the garden.

When it sees an attempt at speaking, His name flees so that you cannot say, "So-and-so will flee."

He will flee from you so that if you draw His image, the image will fly from the tablet, the expression will flee from the heart.

117

What king is He who fashions a king out of dust, for the sake of one or two beggars makes Himself a beggar!

He acts the mendicant like the poor and wretched with His *Give God a loan,* that He may give you a kingdom and fashion a throne.

He passes by the dead and bestows life on the dead, He looks upon pain and contrives a cure for the pain.

When He congeals the wind He makes of the wind water, when He causes the water to boil He fashions out of it air.

5 Look not meanly on the world, for that the world is perishing, for afterwards He will fashion it into an eternal world.

Men marvel at the alchemy which converts copper into gold; regard the copper that every instant fashions alchemy!

If there are a thousand locks on your heart, do not fear; seek the shop of love which the Sweetheart fashions.

He who, without pen and implement, in the idol-house fashions for us a thousand beauteous forms,

Has fashioned for us a thousand Lailās and Majnūns—what form is it that God fashions for the sake of God!

10 If your heart is of iron, weep not for its hardness, for the polishing of His bounty is making it into a mirror of purity.

When you cut away from your friends and go beneath the dust, He will make of snakes and ants fair-featured companions.

Did not Moses fashion the serpent into a succour and a support? Does not He every moment fashion fidelity out of very cruelty?

Look this instant into the grave of your body, what heart-ravishing phantasms He momently fashions there!

When you cleave open your breast, then you see nothing—lest any man should prate idly, saying, "Where does He fashion them?"

15 The proverb says, "Eat the grapes and enquire not of the garden"; God fashions out of stone two hundred fountains of contentment.

Look inside the stone, and there is no trace of the water; it is from the Unseen that He fashions, not out of low and high.

Out of the unconditioned came this conditioned, for out of No He fashions a myriad sayers of Yes.

Behold two rivers of light flowing from two pieces of fat; marvel not that He fashions a stave into a serpent.

Examine these two ears; where is the amber of speech? Marvel at Him who makes of a hole amber!

20 He gives the house a soul and makes it a master; when He slays the master, He fashions of him again a house;

Though the form of the master has descended under the dust,
He fashions the heart of the master into an abode of majesty.

To the eye of men who worship form, the master departed, but
He is fashioning the master a cloak of a different design.

Be silent, speak less with the tongue of praise and paean, that
God may fashion you into paean and praise.

118

On the day of death, when my bier is on the move, do not
suppose that I have any pain at leaving this world.

Do not weep for me, say not "Alas, alas!" You will fall into
the devil's snare—that would indeed be alas!

When you see my hearse, say not "Parting, parting!" That
time there will be for me union and encounter.

When you commit me to the grave, say not "Farewell, fare-
well!" For the grave is a veil over the reunion of paradise.

5   Having seen the going-down, look upon the coming-up; how
should setting impair the sun and the moon?

To you it appears as setting, but it is a rising; the tomb appears
as a prison, but it is release for the soul.

What seed ever went down into the earth which did not grow?
Why do you doubt so regarding the human seed?

What bucket ever went down and came not out full? Why
this complaining of the well by the Joseph of the spirit?

When you have closed your mouth on this side, open it on
that, for your shout of triumph will echo in the placeless air.

119

Love took away sleep from me—and love takes away sleep,
for love purchases not the soul and mind for so much as half a
barleycorn.

Love is a black lion, thirsty and blood-drinking, it pastures
only on the blood of lovers.

It clings to you in affection, and drags you to the snare; when you have fallen in, then it looks on from afar.

Love is a tyrannous prince, an unscrupulous police officer, it tortures and strangles the innocent.

5 Whoso falls into Love's hands weeps like a cloud; whoso dwells afar from Love freezes like snow.

Every instant Love shatters a thousand bowls into fragments, every moment stitches and rends a thousand garments.

Love causes a thousand eyes to weep, and goes on laughing; Love slays miserably a thousand souls, and counts them as one.

Though the simurgh flies happily in Mount Qāf, when it sees Love's snare it falls, and flies no more.

No man escapes from Love's cords by deceit or madness, no reasoning man escapes from its snare by intelligence.

10 My words are disordered because of Love, else I would have shown you the ways Love travels;

I would have shown you how Love seizes the lion, I would have shown you how Love hunts the prey.

120

Henceforward the nightingale in the garden will tell of us, it will tell of the beauty of that heart-ravishing Beloved.

When the wind falls upon the head of the willow and it begins to dance, God alone knows what things it says to the air.

The plane-tree understands a little about the meadow's burning, it lifts up two broad hands sweetly and prays.

I ask the rose, "From whom did you steal that beauty?" The rose laughs softly out of shame, but how should she tell?

5 Though the rose is drunk, it is not dissolute like me, that it should tell you the secret of the intoxicated narcissus.

When you seek secrets, go amongst the drunkards, for the tipsy head shamelessly tells the secret.

Inasmuch as wine is the daughter of the vine and the family of generosity, it has opened the purse's mouth and speaks of lavishness;

Especially the wine of the heavenly trellis from the All-generous Almighty; haply God will speak of its lavishness and generosity.

That new wine ferments from the breast of the gnostic, out of the depths of his body's vat it invites you to the feast.

10   Since the breast gives milk, it can also give wine; from the breast its flowing fountain tells a pretty tale.

When that spirit becomes more intoxicated, it stakes its cloak, lays down cap, and abandons this gown.

When the reason drinks blood-red wine recklessly, it opens its mouth and tells the mysteries of Majesty.

Be silent, for no one will believe you; bad copper swallows not what the philosopher's stone says.

Bear tidings to Tabriz, Pride of the World; perchance our Shams-i Dīn will speak your praise.

I 2 I

Love for you makes me oblivious to my own kindred, for love of you has rooted up the foundations of well-being;

For Love desires only ruination of one's affairs, for Love accepts counsel from no calamity.

What place is there for wealth and fair repute and respect and pomp? What is household and safety, what family or children?

When Love's sword snatches away the lover's soul, a thousand lay down their sacred lives in thanks therefor.

5   What, the desire of love for you, and then the fear of ruination? You with purse fastened, and then the love for that sugar lip?

Draw back your head and sit in the corner of safety—the short hand aspires not to the tall cypress.

Go! In all your life you have not caught the scent of Love; this is not Love, this is reason self-satisfied.

What is it to exercise patience and snatch the skirt out of temptation, seated to see what will come down from heaven for a few days?

Love's fire arrived and consumed all that is beside Him; since all is consumed, sit content and laugh gaily!

10   Especially the love of that One the like of whom, from Alast till now, has never been so devoted to chastity.

If you say, "I have seen Him," for God's sake open another eye and close these twain;

For by this glance, thousands of thousands like me and you in both worlds have been destroyed and blinded for ever.

If to my eye other than that Beauty should come, may my two eyes be gouged out with an axe!

The sight of all heroic men has proved powerless; how should the slothful attain the Beauty and Majesty of the King?

15 Would that God had rent the veil of being, even as 'Alī the Lion rent the gates of Khaibar,

That the eye might have seen how for a thousand years, five times a day, the drums are beaten for him on the other side!

I 2 2

Love for you took away my rosary and gave verses and songs; I cried "No strength (save with God)" and repented oft, but my heart did not heed.

At Love's hand I became a singer of odes, hand-clapping; love for you consumed reputation and shame and all that I possessed.

Once I was chaste and self-denying and firm-footed as a mountain; what mountain is there that your wind did not carry away like chaff?

If I am a mountain, yet I hold the echo of your voice; and if I am chaff, in your fire I am reduced to smoke.

5 When I saw your being, I became nonexistent out of shame; out of the love of this nonexistence the world of soul came into being.

Wherever nonexistence comes, existence diminishes—brave nonexistence, from which, when it came, existence augmented!

Heaven is blue, earth like a blind squatter on the road; he who beholds your moon escapes from blind-and-blue.

The likeness of the soul of a great saint hidden in the body of the world is the likeness of Aḥmad the Messenger amidst the Guebres and Jews.

To praise you in reality is to praise oneself, for he who praises the sun thereby praises his own eyes.

10   Your praise is as the sea, our tongue is a ship; the soul voyages
on the sea, and its end is praiseworthy.
      The tender care of the sea is for me like wakeful fortune; why
should I grieve, if my eye is stained with sleep?

123

At the night prayer, when the sun declines to sinking, this way
of the senses is closed and the way to the Unseen is opened.
      The angel of sleep then drives forward the spirits, even as the
shepherd who watches over his flock.
      To the placeless, towards the spiritual meadows, what cities
and what gardens he there displays to them!
      The spirit beholds a thousand marvellous forms and shapes,
when sleep excises from it the image of the world.
5   You might say that the spirit was always a dweller there, it
remembers not this world, and its weariness does not increase.
      Its heart so escapes from the load and burden for which it
trembled here, that no care for it gnaws at it any more.

124

A little apple, half red and half yellow, made tale of rose and
saffron.
      When the lover became parted from the beloved, the beloved
carried off the airs of pride, the lover the pains.
      These two contrary hues through a single separation have
displayed on the cheeks of both.
      It is not appropriate for the beloved's cheeks to be yellow; for
the lover to be red and fat is unseemly.
5   Since the beloved has begun to show airs, endure his airs,
lover, and do not battle against them.
      I am like a thorn and my master is as the rose; they are twain,
in reality they are one.
      He is as the sun, and I am the shadow; his is the heat of
continuance, mine the cold.

Goliath went out against Toliath; David *measured well the links.*

The heart was born of the body but is the king of the body, even as man is born of woman.

Again within the heart there is a heart hidden, like a horseman hidden in dust;

The stirring of the dust is caused by the horseman—it is he who caused this dust to dance.

No chess is it, for you to apply your thoughts; with trust in God fling away your counter like dice.

Shams-i Tabrīz is the sun of the heart; that heat nurtured the fruits of the heart.

125

My verse resembles the bread of Egypt—night passes over it, and you cannot eat it any more.

Devour it the moment it is fresh, before the dust settles upon it.

Its place is the warm climate of the heart; in this world it dies of cold.

Like a fish it quivered for an instant on dry land, another moment and you see it is cold.

Even if you eat it imagining it is fresh, it is necessary to conjure up many images.

What you drink is really your own imagination; it is no old tale, my good man.

126

Take heed, for the time of men of fortitude has come, the hour of hardship and testing has come.

In such a time covenants are broken, when the knife reaches to the bone.

Covenants and oaths become very weak when the affairs of a man threaten his life.

Ha, my heart, do not make yourself weak; make your heart
strong, for the time for that has come.

5   Laugh like red gold in the fire, that men may say, "The gold of
the mine has come."

Eager and cheerful before the sword of doom, cry aloud, "The
champion has come."

Be with God and pray to Him for help, for replenishment has
come from heaven.

O God, shake the sleeve of bounty, since Your servant has
come to the threshold.

Like an oyster shell we have our mouths open, for the cloud of
Your pearl-scattering grace has come.

10   Many a dry thorn there is out of whose heart a rosegarden has
emerged in Your protection.

I have pointed to You, because from You signless joys have
come.

It is the time of compassion and sympathy, for a very heavy
blow has come upon me.

Abābīl! Take heed, for the army of the Elephant without
bounds has come against the Kaaba.

Reason says to me, "Be silent! Enough; for God who knows
the Unseen has come."

15   I held my peace, O God; but without my will lamentation
mounted up from my soul.

Thou threwest not when thou threwest is also of God—the
arrow which suddenly came from this bow.

127

Someone said, "Master Sanā'ī is dead." The death of such a
master is no small thing.

He was not chaff which flew on the wind, he was not water
which froze in the cold;

He was not a comb that split on a hair, he was not a seed
crushed by the earth.

He was a treasure of gold in this dust bowl, for he reckoned
both worlds at one barleycorn.

The earthly mould he flung to the earth, the soul of reason he carried to the heavens.

The second soul of which men know nothing—we talk ambiguously—he committed to the Beloved.

The pure wine mingled with the wine-dregs, rose to the top of the vat and separated from the dregs.

They meet together on the journey, dear friend, native of Marghaz, of Rayy, of Rum, Kurd;

Each one returns to his own home—how should silk be compared with striped cloth?

10 Be silent, like (a letter's) points, inasmuch as the King has erased your name from the volume of speech.

128

Ah, what was there in that light-giving candle that it set fire to the heart, and snatched the heart away?

You who have set fire to my heart, I am consumed, O friend; come quickly, quickly!

The form of the heart is not a created form, for the beauty of God manifested itself from the cheek of the heart.

I have no succour save in his sugar, I have no profit save in his lip.

5 Remember him who one dawn released this heart of mine from the chain of your tress.

My soul, the first time I saw you my soul heard something from your soul.

When my heart drank water from your fountain it drowned in you, and the torrent snatched me away.

129

A sour-faced one has come—perchance is he the bitter winter cold? Pour a winecup over his head, saki, sweet as sugar.

Either give him wine from the bottle, or send him on his way now, for it is not pleasant, boy, for an efreet to be amongst rose-cheeked beauties.

Bestow the prophetic wine, so that the ass may not continue in assishness; from Jesus' wine two wings forthwith sprout on the ass.

If a sober heart enters the assembly of the drunkards, do not let him; you know that, in the state of drunkenness, good and evil befall the drunkard.

5   Watchman, sit by the door, give not admittance to our assembly save to the heart-aflame lover from whom comes the odour of a burning heart.

If you want a hand, he gives a foot; if you want a foot, he lays down his head; if you want to borrow a hoe, instead of the hoe he brings an axe.

Since I became immersed in wine I have become without shame and heart; the shield is no protection to me, I am myself as a shield before the sword.

I desire a chanter, a living water of life, to set fire to sleep and to utter this melody till dawn.

If you find one sober vein in me, pluck it out; if a man has not been a lion catcher of God, reckon him a dog in this path.

10   Some folk dissolute and drunk and gay, some folk slaves to the five and the six; these are apart and those are apart, these are other and those are other.

I have consumed beyond measure, for I have lost the treasure; bind my hand, bind my mouth—this is how to preserve the drunkard.

Take heed, convert our sting to honey, give ear to our lament; make us senseless like yourself, senseless look upon us.

130

Yesterday at dawn passing by the Beloved said to me, "You are distraught and unaware; how long will this go on?

My cheek is the envy of the rose; and have you filled your eye with heart's blood in quest of the thorn?"

I said, "Before your stature the cypress is but a sapling!" I said, "Before your cheek the heavens' candle is dark!"

I said, "Sky and earth are topsy-turvy on account of you; it is no wonder therefore, if I have no access to you."

He said, "I am your soul and heart; why are you distracted? Say no word, and remain weeping against my silvery bosom."

I said, "You who have robbed my heart and soul of repose, I have not the power to be still." He said at once,

"You are a drop of my sea; why do you utter still? Become drowned, and fill the soul of the oyster shell with pearls."

131

Again in sleep that root of wakefulness gave me the opium of wild commotion and set me reeling.

With a hundred devices I try to be heedless, I make myself to ignore him; that perfect moon comes, holding in his hand such a bowl.

He says to me, "Will you not say how long with those beggarly looks, like every naked unfortunate, you will go on begging at every door?

With this complaining and reviling you are the slave of dervish habit and ewer; if you are true and a man of verity, why are you in this sack?

Kings are put to shame by these things which are born of you; you were an angel—why must you be the plaything of the devil?"

Who knows to speak what he speaks? For the world is not his mate; the universe is blind, and being deaf, to what he discloses and conceals.

If I had the tongue to reveal the Beloved's secret, every soul which heard would burst out of this pass.

On account of that sea-bountiful Beloved my state is very difficult, for my breast is laid waste by that leaping and charging to and fro.

If I tell the believers they will all instantly become infidels, and if I tell the infidels no infidel will remain in the world.

When last night his phantom came in sleep, graciously it enquired of me, "How are you?" I said, "Without you, in dire straits."

If I had a hundred souls, they would all become blood shed in grieving for you, Beloved; your heart is stone, or a mountain of marble!

132

I grant that your prince has gold by the ton; but how happens it that the gold-rich man obtains a cheek like gold?

When they heard complaining from the wretched, frenzied lover, rose and rosebower came out from the earth to behold the spectacle.

Quick, strip off your clothes at once; jump into this pool, that you may escape from your head and the pressure of your turban.

We too like you used to disapprove of this tumult; through a single wink we became thus beguiled by the beloved.

5   How long will you break your lover out of jealous rage? Let be, that this sick heart may utter two or three laments.

No, no, let it not be, for by reason of its wretched lamentation neither earth's people remains, nor the wheeling sky.

Today it were no wonder if that veiled world were not disclosed by leave of the Veiler.

Again this mad heart has broken loose from its chain, torn its collar once more out of passionate love.

Silence! For the indication from the King of Love is thus: "In fortitude seize and compress the throat of your heart and soul!"

133

In this cold and rain the Beloved is sweeter, the Beauty in the bosom, and Love in the brain.

The Beauty in the bosom, and what a beauty! Graceful and fair and supple and fresh and shining-new.

In this cold let us flee to his quarter, for none his like was ever born of mother.

In this snow let us kiss his lips, for snow and sugar refresh the heart.

I have no more strength, I am gone out of hand, they have carried me away and brought me again.

When his phantasm suddenly enters the heart, the heart departs out of its place; God is Most Great!

134

There is a light in the midst of the red hair, transcending eye and imagination and spirit.

Do you desire to stitch yourself to it? Arise, and rend the veil of the carnal soul.

That subtle spirit became a form with eyebrows and eyes and brown skin.

God the Inscrutable disclosed Himself to the form of the Chosen Prophet.

That form of his passed away in the Form, and that eye of his, like the day of resurrection.

Every time he looked upon men, a hundred doors were opened by God.

When the form of the Chosen One passed away, "God is Most Great" seized the world.

135

I have a bad habit; I am weary; pray excuse me. How shall my habit become seemly without your fair face, my beauty?

Without you I am like winter, people are tormented because of me; with you I am as a rosebower, my habit is the habit of spring.

Without you I lack reason, I am weary, everything I say is crooked, I am ashamed of reason and reason is shamefast at the light of your face.

What is the remedy for bad water? To return to the river. What is the remedy for bad habits? To see the beloved's face again.

5   I see the water of the soul imprisoned in this whirlpool of the body; I dig out the earth to make a way to the sea.

You have a potion which you give the despairing, secretly, lest the hopeful, grieving for it, should utter lamentation.

O heart, so much as you are able do not withhold your eye from the Beloved, whether He withdraws from you or draws you into His bosom.

136

Each moment I catch from my bosom the scent of the Beloved; how should I not take my self every night into my bosom?

Last night I was in Love's garden; that desire ran into my head; his sun peeped out of my eye, so that the river began to flow.

Every laughing rose that springs from the bank of that river of love had escaped from the thorn of being and eluded Dhu 'l-Faqār;

Every tree and grass was a-dancing in the meadow, but in the eye of the vulgar was bound and at rest.

5   Suddenly from one side our Cypress appeared, so that the garden was beside itself and the plane-tree clapped its hands.

Face like fire, wine like fire, love afire—all three delightful; soul because of the intermingled fires lamenting, "Whither shall I flee?"

In the world of Divine Unity there is no room for number, but number exists of necessity in the world of five and four.

You may count a myriad sweet apples in your hand; if you want to make one, squeeze them all together.

A myriad grapes went forth from the veil of skin; when skin no more remained, there remained the wine of the Prince.

10   Without counting the letters, behold what is this speech of the heart; unicolority—is it not a form derived from the root of the affair?

Shams-i Tabrīzī is seated like a king, and before him my verses are ranged like willing slaves.

137

Reason is the chain of travellers and lovers, my son; break the chain, and the way is plain and clear ahead, my son.

Reason is a chain, heart a cheat, body a delusion, soul a veil; the way is hidden from all these heavinesses, my son.

When you have risen out of reason, soul, and heart, and you have gone forth, still this certainty and this direct vision is in doubt, my son.

The man who has not departed out of self is not a man, my son; the love which is not of the soul is but a legend, my son.

Set up your breast as a target before the arrow of His decree; be sharp, for the arrow of His decree is already in the bow, my son.

The breast that has been wounded by the striking of the arrow of His tug, on its brow and face are a hundred marks, my son.

If you mount like Idris to the seventh heaven, the love of the Beloved is an excellent ladder indeed, my son.

On every side where a caravan takes its proud way behold love, which is the *qibla* of the caravan, my son.

His love has cast a shadow on the earth like a snare; His huntsmanlike love is in heaven, my son.

o   Enquire not of me concerning love, enquire not of any man, enquire of Love itself; Love in speaking is like a pearl-raining cloud, my son.

Love requires not the interpreter service of me and a hundred like me; concerning realities Love is its own interpreter, my son.

Love is not the business of those asleep or soft and delicate, Love is the business of the brave and of heroes, my son.

Whoso has become the servant of lovers and true ones, he is a king, an emperor, a master of fortune, my son.

Let not this world full of magic spells lure you away from Love, for this faithless world is leaping away from you, my son.

5   If the verses of this ode have become long in its joins, the tune has changed but the meaning is the same, my son.

Take heed, close your mouth and be silent henceforth like an oyster shell, for this tongue of yours is in reality the enemy of the soul, my son.

138

Tonight is a night of union for the stars and of scattering, scattering, since a bride is coming from the skies, consisting of a full moon.

Venus cannot contain herself for charming melodies, like the nightingale which becomes intoxicated with the rose in springtime.

See how the Polestar is ogling Leo; behold what dust Pisces is stirring up from the deep!

Jupiter has galloped his steed against ancient Saturn, saying, "Take back your youth and go, bring good tidings!"

5   Mars' hand, which was full of blood from the handle of his sword, has become life-giving as the sun, the exalted in works.

Since Aquarius has come full of that water of life, the dry cluster of Virgo is raining pearls from him.

The Pleiades (nut) full of goodness fears not Libra and being broken; how should Aries flee away in fright from its mother?

When from the moon the arrow of a glance struck the heart of Sagittarius, he took to night-faring in passion for her, like Scorpio.

On such a festival, go, sacrifice Taurus, else you are crooked of gait in the mud like Cancer.

10   This sky is the astrolabe, and the reality is Love; whatever we say of this, attend to the meaning.

Shams-i Tabrīz, on that dawn when you shine, the dark night is transformed to bright day by your moonlike face.

139

That beauty handed me a broom saying, "Stir up the dust from the sea!"

He then burned the broom in the fire saying, "Bring up the broom out of the fire!"

In bewilderment I made prostration before him; he said, "Without a prostrator, offer a graceful prostration!"

"Ah, how prostrate without a prostrator?" He said, "Unconditionally, without personal impulse."

I lowered my neck and said, "Cut off the head of a prostrator with Dhu 'l-Faqār."

The more he struck with the sword, the more my head grew, till heads a myriad sprouted from my neck;

I was a lamp, and every head of mine was as a wick; sparks flew on every side.

Candles sprang up out of my heads, east to west was filled with the train.

What are east and west in the placeless? A dark bath-stove, and a bath at work.

o You whose temperament is cold, where is the anxiety of your heart? How long this dwelling at rest in these baths?

Go forth from the baths and enter not the stove; strip yourself, and look upon those paintings and figures,

Until you behold the ravishing figures, until you behold the hues of the tulip-bed.

When you have beheld, look towards the window, for that beauty became a beauty through the reflection of the window.

The six directions are the bath, and the window is the placeless; above the window is the beauty of the Prince.

5 Earth and water acquired colour from his reflection, soul rained on Turk and Zanzibari.

The day is gone, and my story has not grown short—O night and day put to shame by his tale!

King Shams al-Dīn-i Tabrīzī keeps me intoxicated, crop-sickness upon crop-sickness.

140

I went there intoxicated and said, "O beauty, when you have maddened me, give ear!"

He replied, "See, in my ear is a ring; become fastened to that ring like a pendant."

I quickly reached out to touch his ring; he struck me saying, "Hold back your hand from me!

You will find the way into this ring only when you become a royal pearl in purity.

5 My golden ring, and then a bead! How should Jesus go up to heaven on an ass?"

141

Joyous spring has arrived and the Beloved's message has come; we are drunk with love and intoxicated and cannot be still.

O my darling one, go forth to the garden, do not leave the beauties of the meadow in expectation.

Strangers from the Unseen have arrived in the meadow; go forth, for it is a rule that "the newcomer is visited."

Following your footsteps the rose has come into the rosebower, to greet and meet you the thorn has become soft of cheek.

5 Cypress, give ear, for the lily in exposition of you has become all tongue by the bank of the river.

The bud was tightly knotted; your grace looses knots; the rose blossoms thanks to you, and scatters its petals over you.

You might say that it is the resurrection, that there have raised their heads from the earth those who rotted in December and January, the dead of yesteryear.

The seed which had died has now found life, the secret which earth held has now become revealed.

The bough which held fruit is glorying for joy, the root which had none is shamefast and ashamed.

10 After all, the trees of the spirit will become even so, the tree of excellent boughs and fortunate will be manifest.

The king of spring has drawn up his army and made his provisions; the jasmine has seized the shield, the green grass Dhu 'l-Faqār.

They say, "We will cut off the head of So-and-so like chives; behold that visibly enacted in the handiwork of the Creator."

Yes; when the succour of divine assistance arrives, Nimrod is brought to destruction by a gnat.

142

Do not slacken the bowstring, for I am your four-feathered arrow; do not turn your face away, for I am a man with one heart, not two-headed.

From you is the striking of the sharp sword, from the heart and soul a hundred consents; I am a man of one word like fate, I am not "if" or "perhaps"!

If you draw Dhu 'l-Faqār I am constant and firm of foot, I do not flee like the wind, I do not die like a spark.

I will surrender my soul to the sword, I will not say alas; God has made me like a shield for the blows of His sword.

Sun, smite with your glow the neck of the night as with a sword; whence comes the darkness of the nights? From the forge of muddy earth.

The body is a mine of endurance, the heart is a mine of gratitude, the bosom is a mine of laughter, the liver is a mine of compassion.

Make your throne, O king, on my head as a cap; tightly draw me into your breast as a garment.

Someone said, "Whence has Love form and hands?" Love is the sprouting-bed of every hand and foot in the forms.

Did not your father and mother play at love for one moment? When they were united, one like you made his appearance.

Do not regard Love, which without hands made your hand a hand, as being without hand or head; look in another fashion.

You who have eyes to see, the colour of all faces, the water of all rivers—know these are Shams-i Ḥaqq, the Pride of Tabriz.

143

He said, "My sugar-sweet lip is worth a treasure of pearls." "Ah, I have no pearls." He said, "You have not? Then buy!

Make a snare for me out of pearls, and if that does not succeed, then borrow. You have mistaken the house, you lover without silver and gold!

You have come to a gambling-match; bring a purse full of gold. Else, leave us and be gone, do not vex and trouble us more.

We are highwaymen, we are renders of garments; if you are one of us, come in, drink and drink deep!

We tear to shreds all snares, we devour all properties; we are sweeter than all others—despite all the blind and deaf."

Those who buy garments are different from those who rend

them; those who rend garments pluck out the mustachios of every garment-buyer.

The Moses of the soul plucked out the mustachios of the Pharaoh of the body, so that the body becomes all soul, every hair-tip alive.

Recognize the travellers on the path of his love by their pallid cheeks; know that the pearls of love are tears, love's silk the heart's blood.

What is the worth of the gold-pale cheek? Say: the ruby of the Beloved. What is the worth of the pearl-like tear? Say: that glance.

10   We are slaves to that saki, till eternity we continue; our world is secure and content, the worldlings are passing by.

Whoever has been born has died and committed his soul to the guardian angel; the lover was born of no man, love has no father.

If you are not of this face, then sit behind like the nape; if you are not the nape, then advance like a shield.

Advance like a shield unconscious, and behold how the conscious ones are struck unconscious by the glance of the Friend's blow.

144

God has written around the cheek of the Beloved the inscription *Therefore take heed* of him, *you who have eyes.*

Since Love devours men, it is necessary for a man to make himself a morsel before man-devouring Love.

You are a sour morsel, and are very long digesting; the saint is a sweet morsel easy to digest.

Do you break the morsel you are, because that mouth is narrow; even three elephants would not devour you, save at three gulps.

5   In face of your greed the elephant itself is a morsel; you are like the abābīl birds which made the elephant their prey.

You were born of non-entity, come after a long famine; to you, fattened bird as food and serpent and snake are the same.

You have come to a hot cauldron; now you burn your mouth, now you blacken your clothes and lips and turban.

With nothing are you sated, like the belly of hell, save perchance the Almighty Creator sets His foot on you,

Even as He sets His foot on the head of hell, and hell proclaims, "Enough, I am full, lift up Your foot!"

God satiates the eye of the saints and the elect, for they are delivered from self and from greed for this carrion.

No greed remains in them for knowledge and science, no desire for paradise; the lion-rider does not seek for ass or camel.

Silence! Were I to count His gifts and donations, resurrection day itself would become giddy and confounded at the tally.

Come, Pride of Tabriz, true Shams al-Dīn; the sun in the spinning skies is your humble slave.

145

Look not for happiness when the Beauty's inclination is set on sorrow, for you are prey in the clutches of a lion, my dear friend.

Though the Beloved sprinkles plaster on your head, welcome that as if it was Tartary musk.

Since within you lurks a hidden enemy, there is no repelling that monster save by harshness.

The man who beats a stick on a rug, it is not aimed at the rug, but the whole purpose is to rid the rug of dust.

Layers of dust are within you, consisting of the veil of egoism; that dust is not got rid of at a single blow;

With each harshness and each blow, little by little that is dispersed from the cheek of the heart, now sleeping, now awake.

If you take flight in sleep, in dreams you will see the cruelty of the Beloved and the execrations of that Benefactor.

Scraping a stick is not in order to destroy the stick, it is for a good purpose in the heart of the carpenter.

For this reason every evil on God's path is good, for that He will show man pure and refined at the end of the affair.

Consider the hide which the tanner rubs in all manner of filth a thousand times over,

So that the inward flaw may go forth from the hide, even though the hide knows naught of little or much.

Sun and Pride of Tabriz, you possess great virtues; make haste, for you have a mighty power in the secrets.

146

If a tree could move on foot or wing, it would not suffer the pain of the saw or the blows of the axe;

And if the sun did not travel on wing and foot all the night, how would the world be illumined at morningtide?

If the salt water did not rise from the sea to the sky, whence would the garden be revived by torrent and rain?

When the drop departed from its homeland and returned, it encountered a shell and became a pearl.

5 Did not Joseph go from his father on a journey, weeping? Did he not on the journey attain felicity and kingdom and victory?

Did not Muṣṭafā go on a journey towards Yathrib, gain sovereignty, and become king of a hundred lands?

And you—if you have no foot, choose to journey into yourself; like a ruby-mine be receptive to a print from the sunbeams.

Make a journey out of self into self, my master, for by such a journey earth became a mine of gold.

Go out of sourness and bitterness towards sweetness, just as a thousand sorts of fruits have escaped out of bitterness.

10 Seek sweetness from the Sun, the Pride of Tabriz, for every fruit gains comeliness from the light of the sun.

147

Look on me, for I shall be your companion in the grave on that night when you pass across from shop and house.

You will hear my greeting in the tomb, and you will be aware that not for a moment you have been veiled from my eyes.

I am like reason and mind within your veil, alike in time of pleasure and happiness and in the hour of pain and weariness.

On the strange night, when you hear the voice familiar, you will escape from the bite of snake and leap away from the horror of ant;

Love's intoxication will bring to your grave, as a gift, wine and mistress and candle and meats and sweets and incense.

On the hour when we light the lamp of the intellect, what a tumult of joy shall go up from the dead in the tombs!

The dust of the graveyard will be confounded by those cries, by the din of the drum of resurrection, the pomp and panoply of the uprising—

Shrouds rent asunder, two ears stopped up in terror; what shall avail brain and ear before the blast of the trumpet?

On whatever side you gaze, you will behold my form, whether you gaze on yourself or towards that uproar and confusion.

o   Flee from squinteyedness, and make good both your eyes, for the evil eye on that day will be far from my beauty.

Beware of mistaking me in a human shape, for the spirit is very subtle, and Love is exceedingly jealous.

What room is there for form, if the felt be a hundredfold? It is the rays of the soul's mirror that pitch the flag visibly.

Beat the drum, and wind towards the minstrels of the city; it is the day of purification to the grown lads of the road of Love.

Had they sought God, instead of morsel and pence, you would not have seen one blind man seated on the edge of the moat.

5   What sort of ogling-house have you opened in our city! Mouth shut, shoot out glances, like light.

148

My bowl has broken, and no wine has remained to me, and I am crop-sick; let Shams-i Dīn set in order my disordered estate—

Prince of the world of vision, lamp of the world of revelation, to whom the spirits make heartfelt obeisance from afar,

That his hand may bring out of the sea of bewilderment a thousand souls and spirits drowned and utterly whelmed.

If heaven and earth were filled with the darkness of unbelief, when he shines, his rays flood all that with light.

5 That pure radiance which the angels discover from him—if it should reach the satans, they would all become houris.

And even if that light belonged not for a single day to the devil, he would veil the devil with the veils of his bountifulness.

On the day of festival, when he begins to dispense, on every side is a marriage feast, in every quarter a wedding party.

From the direction of Tabriz that sun shines—the atoms come to life as at the blast of the trumpet.

Zephyr, for God's sake and by the right of bread and salt—for every dawn I and you have been rejoiced by him—

10 When you come to the end of the frontiers of the unseen world, pass over them, and be not lazy as one sick and suffering.

On that wing which you have gotten from him fly; for a thousand years' journey will not be far from your wing.

Fly; and when your wing becomes weary, prostrate yourself for the sake of my state, weary of soul and sundered of heart;

Tell him with tears that since the time of our separation, my day has become black and my hairs camphor-white.

You are he who dips in the sea of compassion all the sinners of the world, and makes them forgiven.

15 If the seeing eye cannot penetrate to your soul, he who has no eye may truly be excused.

So contrive by entreaty as to bring the dust of his feet to the eye, for this sickness is becoming gangrenous.

And when, zephyr, you return prospering from this journey, you will stir up commotion and sparks indeed in existence and nonexistence alike.

When you bring me his eye salve, may a thousand new compassions be upon your soul for centuries beyond reckoning!

149

Minstrel of the lovers, shake the string, strike fire into believer and infidel!

Silence is not the proper course of love; unveil the face of welfare.

Until the infant in the cradle weeps, how shall the anxious mother give it milk?

Whatever is other than the phantom of the Beloved is the thorn of Love, even if it be a rosebower.

Minstrel, when you have reached to dilate my heart, have a care; you have set your foot in blood—

Set your foot slowly, lest a drop of the heart's blood splash out on the wall.

Minstrel, observe well the wounds of the heart; so long as they are not conscious of their pain, be at ease.

Minstrel, mention the name of the beloved who has robbed our heart of fortitude and quietude.

What have I said? Where has a heart remained still? If my heart were a mountain, it had gone out of control.

Speak his name, and name me less, that I may nickname you "Excellent of speech."

When I speak of how he moves, where does my heart go? Brave movement indeed!

Shams-i Tabrīz, you are the Jesus of the age; in your age there is such a sick one.

150

Who has compassion on a friend? A friend likewise. Who hears the sigh of the sick? The sick.

Where are the tears of sympathetic spring, that they may fill the thorn's skirt with roses?

Mention often the demolisher of joy; give ear to pitiless autumn.

The cave becomes paradise, when he is in it: *the second of two, when the two were in the Cave.*

Heaven splits in two at the sigh of a lover; the lamentation of lovers is not to be despised.

Heaven revolves for the sake of lovers; on account of love the sky spins around,

Not for the sake of baker and smith, not for the sake of carpenter and druggist.

The skies rotate about love; rise, that we may also circle around.

Consider who said, "But for thee I would not have created";
Aḥmad the Chosen is the mine of love.

10   For a while let us circle about loverhood; how long shall we
circle about this carrion?

Where is the eye to behold the spirits, putting their heads out
from door and wall?

Door and wall tell subtleties, fire and earth and water rehearse
a tale;

Like the balance, the yardstick and the touchstone they are
without tongue, yet arbiters of the market.

Lover, circle about like the sky, silent from speaking, and
altogether speech.

151

So drunk am I, so drunk am I today that I have leaped out of
the hoop today.

Such a thing as never enters the mind, even so am I, even so
am I today.

In spirit I departed to the heaven of Love, even though in
form I am in this low world today.

I took reason by the ear and said, "Reason, go out, for I have
escaped from you today.

5   Reason, wash your hands of me, for I am joined with the mad
lover today.

That Joseph gave into my hand an orange; as a result, I have
wounded both my hands today."

That jug full of wine has brought me to such a state that I
have broken so many jars today.

I do not know where I am, but it is a blessed station in which I
am today.

Good fortune came coquettishly to my door; out of drunken-
ness I closed the door to him today.

10   When he returned, I kept running after him, I did not sit
down for a moment today.

Since *We are nearer* has been realized, I will not worship
myself any more today.

Do not tie up that tress, Shams al-Dīn-i Tabrīz, for I am like a
fish in this net today.

152

The love of that cherisher of lovers has come to his own house; Love has in form-conceiving a form melting all forms.

You have come to your own house; welcome, enter! Your coming is with joy; enter by the door of the heart, run to the vestibule of the soul.

Every mote of my being is in love with your sun; take heed, for motes have long transaction with the sun.

See how before the window the motes gracefully suspended beat; whoever has the sun for a *qibla* prays after this fashion.

In the concert of the sun these motes are like Sufis; no one knows to what recitation, to what rhythm, to what harmony.

In every heart there is a different note and rhythm, all stamping feet outwardly, and the minstrels hidden like a secret.

Loftier than all is our inward concert, our particles dancing therein with a hundred kinds of glory and pride.

Shams-i Tabrīzī, you are the sultan of the sultans of the soul; no Maḥmūd like you ever came into being, nor like me any Ayāz.

153

Night is broad and long for the sake of lovers and thieves; ho, come, strumpet night, and do the business of both!

I steal carnelians and pearls from the sultan's treasury, I am not mean that I should steal the draper's cloth.

Within the veil of the nights there are subtle thieves who by cunning find a way to the roof of the house of mystery.

My ambition in night-faring and knavery is nothing less than the king's treasury and the carnelian of that king of glory.

The cheek before whose onslaught night remains no more in the world—brave lamp, which lights the sun and fashions the moon!

All the needs of men are granted on the Night of Power, for Power attained that exaltation from a full moon like you.

You are all, and beyond all what else is there, that it should enter the imagination that anyone is your peer?

Ho, pass away from this; open wide your ears, for I am beginning a tale entirely rare and strange.

Since you have not seen Messiah, give ear to the legend; fly like a white falcon towards the falcon-drum.

10   Since you are a coin of red gold, receive the seal of the king; if you are not red gold, then why all this snipping?

In the time when you became a treasure you did not realize that, wherever a treasure is, the informer sets to work.

Bring your treasure, and play no tricks, for you will not escape by vapouring and prostration and commemoration and abstinence and prayer.

Do you steal, and then sit in the corner of the mosque saying, "I am the Junaid of the age, the Bā Yazīd of supplication"?

Give back the cloth, then get on with your abstinence; do not make feeble excuses and babble your tale.

15   Hush your pretexts, for in this station men do not purchase a single grain by dissimulation and artful trickery.

Seize the skirt of felicity of Shams-i Tabrīzī, that your perfection may be embroidered from the magic of his sleeve.

154

Sour-faced one, in my presence you spoke evil of me; the mouth of the vulture always smells of carrion.

Your filthy words became apparent in your face; vileness is ever manifest in the face and complexion of the nobody.

I have a Friend and Beloved, so go on grinding away at death and enmity; take heed, the ocean was never defiled by the mouth of any dog.

Though the Holy City has become filled with Frankish pigs, after all how has that brought the Holy Temple a bad name?

5   This is the face of the mirror; Joseph shines in it; the back, however that it is gilded, is a stranger.

If the bat thinks evil, the sun is not grieved—how is the sun impaired, if the shadow is upside down?

Jesus was a laugher, John the Baptist a frowner; the former laughed out of trust, the latter frowned from fear.

They said, "O Lord, which of these two is better in Your eyes? Which of these two is better in the well-founded path?"

God said, "He is superior who thinks better thoughts of Me; the good thoughts of the sinner leave him not defiled."

o You are a frowner not out of fear and religious aspiration, you are pale from envy or dark red from gloating.

Neither of these gets anywhere, they are proper only to the fire; woe to him in whom envy is rooted!

Let it go from your hand; *cursed* is it; whoever is enemy of the moon has only shadows.

Know for sure, O sun, that bats are your enemies, they are a disgrace to all birds, fellow-prisoners in *brooding night.*

The sun's enemy is *docked,* that rank does not remain to him; how long shall the mote there remain if it falls into the eye?

155

Consorts of the Moon are your two Mars, which are those two eyes of yours, Darling; with that Hārūt and Mārūt of yours draw the litigious ones to Babylon.

Solomon, with that ring (for you are the sealing of all the fair ones) by force drag in chains all the divs and peris.

You have opened the treasure of beneficence for the sake of jinns and men; draw the likeness of *We have given thee* over the needy beggar.

Illumine the body with the spirit, root up envy utterly; fix the gaze on the orient skies, draw the reason into problems.

When the lip recites *Praise,* give it dessert and wine unlimited; when it recites *Nor those astray,* do you draw it into guiding proofs.

When the soul hurries towards you, give it a candle to find the way; when it seeks your sun, draw it like the moon into the "houses."

Give the crop-sick lover the wine of Kai-Kā'ūs' cup; draw before the thoughts of the man of reason hairsplitting and craft.

With the advancing of your favours draw the spirit and make it receptive; draw your acceptance and investiture towards the receptive soul.

To the prisoner of pain and regret give the message of *Do not despair;* draw him slain of love for your beauty from this slaying-place to the slayer.

10   If this body is infidel at heart, propose "testimony" to it; and if
this spirit is fruitless, what matters that? Draw it to the fruit.

Quicken it, and if you cannot, make Messiah your deputy;
grant it union, or if you grant it not, draw it by your grace to the
Lord of grace.

Earthy one, the earth trembled when it saw that holiness and
purity; recite *When it is shaken,* draw the vision into trembling.

Make an end of it, ho, at once, for you are the King of State
and Word; whoever proffers speech, do you draw a line over
speech and speaker.

156

The fair one whom I am seeking with all my soul I do not see
amongst those present here.

Where has he gone? He is not amongst those present; I do not
see any sign of him in this assembly.

I am casting my gaze in every direction and every place; I do
not see any trace of his rosebower.

Moslems, where has he gone, that illustrious one whom I used
to behold in the midst like a candle?

5   Speak his name; for whoever has spoken his name, his bones
will not crumble in the tomb.

Blessed is the man who has kissed his hand; at the time of
death his mouth has become sweet.

Shall I give thanks for his countenance, or his character? For
the world beholds none his like.

If earth does not find his form, what matters it, seeing that his
heaven revolves in this love?

Speak the nicknames of Shams al-Dīn-i Tabrīz; do not keep
him concealed from the ears of the yearners.

157

Last night I went into the midst of the assembly of my king; I
saw my soul in a beaker in the hand of the saki.

I said to him, "O soul of the soul of the sakis, for God's sake fill me a measure, and do not break your pledge."

Smiling sweetly he said, "Noble sir, I do you service; I respect you by the right and respect of my faith."

He brought a cup and kissed it and placed it in my hand, full of wine shining like his own shining cheeks.

5   I prostrated before him and drew the bowl to me; the wine lighted a fire in me from its own brazier.

When the saki had poured continuously and dispensed for me many glasses after that wise, that wine like red gold transported me to its own quarry.

I saw my garden fresh and gay with the rose of his cheek; I saw my bread well baked with his hyacinthine brow.

Let every man find his own fortune and portion in a tavern; who am I? I have found true sympathy to belong to me.

10   I saw Bū Lahab there biting hard his hand, Bū Huraira putting his hand in his own wallet;

Bū Lahab was like the back (and no back sees the face), Bū Huraira turning his face to his own moon and seventh heaven;

Bū Lahab plunged in thought, seeking proof and demonstration, Bū Huraira his own proof and his own demonstration.

Not every jar is suitable for wine; beware, stop up the jar, that the saki may produce another jar from his own cellar.

I make this enough, that the Prince of the Assembly may tell you the tale of his own myriad secret assemblies.

158

I am you, you are I, O friend; do not depart from your own breast; do not deem yourself other, do not drive yourself from your own door.

Do not mislead head and foot through your endless temptation, that as one bewildered I should stamp the foot of cruelty on my own head.

The one who like a shadow is never apart from your form, is I; do not, beloved, draw your dagger against your shadow.

O tree, in every direction of which there are thousands of

shadows, cherish the shadows and do not cut them off from their source.

5   Hide all the shadows and naught them in the light; disclose the countenance of the sun of your radiant cheek.

The heart's kingdom has become disordered through your two-heartedness; mount the throne, do not step down from your own pulpit.

"Reason is the crown"—so 'Alī spoke in a similitude; bestow on the throne a new jewel out of your own essence.

159

My drunkenness of today is not like yesterday's drunkenness; do you not believe me? Take a glass, and drink!

I am drowned in wine; the waters have carried away my reason. Intellect said, "Farewell, I will not become sober again."

Reason and intellect have departed in madness out of the world, like a pot overbrimming when it boils beyond measure.

This mad, intoxicated heart burst its bonds and escaped; do not argue with the drunkards—say nothing; depart; keep silent.

5   At dawn the watchman said to me from the ladder, "Last night I heard an uproar proceeding from the seventh heaven.

Saturn said to Venus, 'Strike your plectrum more gently. Leo, seize Taurus by the horns and milk him.'

See how as a result of terror the milk in Taurus' nipples has turned to blood! Behold how the Leo of the skies out of fear has become like a mouse!

Leo, charge fiercely; how long will you flee like a cur? Make display, O moon-faced one; how long will you veil your face?

Open your eyes to the six directions, behold the glittering of the light; open your ears to heaven, you whose eyes have become ears.

10   Hear the greeting from the Soul, that you may escape from speech; gaze upon the Form-fashioner, that you may escape from the forms."

I said to him, "Master, go, say, let what will be be; I am pure and newly free, slave to the dregs-seller."

Fear and hope for you are assigned to the reason; wild crea-
tures are the game for your grain and snare.

Since the dregs of his anguish have taken me into protection,
speak not to me of these things; that task is yours—do you
labour!

160

When union with the Beloved showed itself to Manṣūr, it
was right that the gallows should bring him to the heart's Origin.

I snatched a cap's length from his robe; his cap's length
consumed my reason and head and foot.

I broke off a thorn from the top of the wall of his garden;
what itching and questing is in my heart from that thorn of his!

Since one morning through his wine this heart became a
lion-taker, it is only meet that it should be smitten by the
monster of separation from him.

5   Though heaven's colt appeared refractory and untamed, it was
tethered and headstalled by the hand of His love.

Though reason is high-ranking and very learned, its gown and
turban have been pawned for the cup of love.

Many a heart came seeking refuge from His love; dragging it
along He dragged it to Him, and gave it no quarter.

One cold day a fur coat was in a river; I said to a naked man,
"Jump in and seek, and bring it out!"

It was not a fur coat, it was a bear in the river; it had fallen in,
and the current was carrying it along.

10 The man entered eagerly and reached the skin of the bear;
that eagerness made him prisoner in the bear's arms.

I said to him, "Let go the fur coat, come back! How long and
far you have remained through toiling and battling with it!"

He said, "Go; the coat has so seized me that I have no hope of
escape from its powerful clutches.

Every moment it immerses me a thousand times; there is no
escape from its liver-squeezing claws."

Silence, of stories enough; just give a hint; what need has the
reason for long volumes?

161

They say, "The king of love is not faithful." Lies! They say, "Your night will never have a dawn." Lies!

They say, "Why do you slay yourself for love's sake? There is no survival after the body's death." Lies!

They say, "Your tears shed in love are vain; once the eyes are closed, there will be no encounter." Lies!

They say, "When we have gone outside the cycle of time, beyond this soul of ours will not travel." Lies!

5 Those persons who have not escaped from fancy say, "The stories of the prophets were all mere fancies." Lies!

Those persons who have not gone on the right way say, "The servant has no way to come to God." Lies!

They say, "He who knows all secrets tells not the servant the secrets and mysteries of the Unseen without intermediary!" Lies!

They say, "They open not to the servant the heart's secret, and He does not graciously carry the servant up to heaven." Lies!

They say, "That one who has earth in his composition will never be familiar with the heavenly host." Lies!

10 They say, "The pure soul will never fly on the wings of love out of this earthly nest to the free air." Lies!

They say, "That sun of God will never bring retribution for the several atoms' weight of evil and good of men." Lies!

Keep silent from speaking; and if anyone says to you, "Speech has no other expression but letters and sounds"—Lies!

162

We two or three gay reprobates have gathered together on this side like camels, face to face, muzzles plunged in the provender.

From left and right every camel is coming, raging with desire, lips thrust out like camels, bringing up foam.

Do not worry; not every camel finds the way to this sheepcote, for they are in the lowlands and we are on top of the mountain.

How shall any attain the mountaintop by stretching up his

neck? Even though they bark like dogs, we will not worry about their barking.

5   If the world becomes all sea, enter the ark of Noah; how should Noah's ark be overwhelmed and destroyed?

We are a mine of emeralds, a bane to the eye of the snake; he who is bitten by sorrow, his portion is "Woe is me!"

All the world is full of grief in quest of rank and money; we are happy and glad and revered, drunk with joy in this protection.

The gnostics have become drunk; minstrel of gnosis, come, quickly utter a quatrain, come forward, take the tambourine.

Cast wind into the forest, blow on the head of cypress and willow, that willow and plane-tree rank by rank may toss their heads.

10 When the willow is dry and bald, it has neither leaves nor fruit; how should it move its head to the breath and wind of *Do not fear?*

The remedy for the dry and succourless is the blast divine, for He is engaged on action one by one, He is not weak and contemptible.

The dry palm-tree gave fruit to a Mary by the fiat of God; the dead found life anew from the breath divine.

If the fool wags his chin, do not lose the path of Love; choose the trade of Love, count as folly all other trades.

When you complete one ode, recite the praises of Shams-i Dīn and recall Tabriz, despite the villainous adversary.

163

I have no need of wine, I am indifferent to lees and pure liquor; I thirst for my own blood, the time of battle has come.

Draw the sharp sword, shed the blood of the envious until the head without the body circumambulates about its own body.

Make a mountain of skulls, make a sea of our blood, that earth and sand may drink blood in great gulps.

You who are aware of my heart, go, do not stop up my mouth, else my heart will split, the blood will leap out of the rent.

5   Do not listen to the tumult, show no special favour; rulership
and authority are not so hand-woven.

I will enter the heart of the fire, I will become a morsel for the
fire; foretelling what, have they cut the navel of the sulphur-like
soul?

Fire is our child, it thirsts and is in bondage to us; we two are
becoming one so that no difference may prevail.

Why does it crackle and smoke? Because two-colouredness is
still there; when it becomes fuel, it no longer crackles boastfully.

Or if it leaps half-ablaze, it now becomes a coal, heart-athirst
and black-faced, seeking union and marriage.

10   The fire says, "Go, you are black and I am white." The fuel
says, "You are burnt, I am preserved."

This side of it no face, that side of it no face, making seclusion
in blackness between the two friends;

Like an exiled Moslem, no way for him to come to people nor
to emperor, left on one side like the fringe of a garment.

Rather, he is like the 'Anqā which was greater than all the
birds, but having no way to the sky, remained upon that moun-
tain of Qāf.

What am I to say to you? For you are fixed in your grief for
bread, your back curved like a *lām*, your heart constricted like a
kāf.

15   Ho, trouble-seeker, dash that pitcher against a rock, that I may
not draw river-water, that I may not suck it up.

I will abandon water-carrying, I will drown myself in the sea,
far from warfare and conflict, unaware of any description,

Like pure spirits under the earth, their bodies like a bride with
earth on them for a coverlet.

164

Look at that false prince with his little horse and little saddle,
knavish and scoundrelly, his head bound in cloth of gold;

Since he disbelieves in death, he says, "Where, where is
doom?" Death comes to him from all six directions and says,
"Here am I!"

Doom says to him, "Donkey, where now is all that galloping about? Those moustaches, that arrogant nose, that pride, that wrath?

Where is the beautiful idol, where happiness? To whom have you given your coverlet? A brick is now your pillow, your mattress the earth."

5 Bid farewell to eating and sleeping; go seek the true religion, that you may be a prince of eternity without your little laws and customs.

Do not unsoul this soul; do not convert this bread to dung, O you who have flung the pearl into the bottom of the dung.

Know that we are attached to dung for the pearl's sake, O soul; be broken, and seek the pearl, proud and conceited one.

When you see a man of God, act like a man and offer him service; when you experience anguish and affliction, do not furrow your brow.

This is my lampoon, O body, and that prince of mine is also I; how long will you go on speaking of little *sins* and *shins*?

Shams al-Haqq-i Tabrīzī, you are yourself the water of life; what shall discover that water, save the tearful eye?

165

What, loverhood and then concern for name and shame? That should not be; Love's village is stone on stone!

If you become lame from everything, depart far away; what, a far and stony way, and a lame man?

If death is a man, let him come before me that I may draw him fondly and tightly into my bosom;

I will carry off from him a soul without hue and scent, he will seize from me a cloak of many colours.

5 Impose on your soul the cruelty and tyranny of the Beloved; or if you will not, then welcome to war and war!

If you do not desire the scraping of His polishing, then be like a mirror full of rust.

Lay your hand on your eye and say, "With all my eye!" Open your eye; do not gaze distraught and stupefied.

166

I cried out at midnight, "Who is in this house of the heart?" He said, "It is I, by whose countenance the sun and the moon are put to shame."

He said, "Why is this house of the heart full of all sorts of images?" I said, "These are the reflections of You, whose face is the envy of Chigil."

He said, "What is this other image, full of the heart's blood?" I said, "This is the image of me, heart wounded and feet in the mire."

I bound the neck of my soul and brought it before Him as a token: "It is a sinner of love; do not acquit your sinner."

5   He gave me the end of a thread, a thread full of mischief and craft; he said, "Pull, that I may pull, pull and at the same time do not break."

From that tent of the soul the form of my Turk flashed out fairer than before; I reached my hand towards him; He struck my hand, saying, "Let go!"

I said, "You have turned harsh, like So-and-so." He said, "Know that I am harsh for a good purpose, not harsh out of rancour and spite.

Whoever enters in saying, 'It is I,' I strike him on the brow, for this is the sanctuary of Love, animal, it is not a sheepcote."

Ṣalāḥ-i Dil u Dīn is truly the image of that Turk; rub your eyes, and behold the image of the heart, the image of the heart.

167

Why does the soul not take wing, when from the presence of Glory the address of grace like sugar comes to the soul saying, "Come up"?

How should a fish not leap nimbly from the dry land into the water, when the sound of waves reaches its ear from the limpid sea?

Why should the falcon not fly from the quarry towards the

king, when it hears from drum and drumstick the tidings *Return?*

Why should not every Sufi begin to dance like a mote in the sun of immortality, that it may deliver him from decay?

Such grace and beauty and loveliness and life-bestowing—can any man dispense with Him? What misery and error!

Fly, fly, O bird, to your origin, for you have escaped from the cage and your feathers and wings are outspread.

Journey away from the brackish water towards the water of life; return to the high table of the soul from the porter's lodge.

Off, off! For we too, O soul, are arriving from this world of separation to that world of union.

How long like children in this earthly world shall we fill our skirts with dust and stones and crocks?

10   Let us leave go of earth and fly heavenwards, let us flee from childhood to the banquet of men.

Look not to see how the earthly mould has put you in a sack; split the sack and lift your head out of the sack.

Take from the air this book in your right hand; you are not a child, not to know your right from your left.

God said to Reason's messenger, "Lift up your foot!", to the hand of Death, "Beat the ear of concupiscence!"

A call came to the spirit, "Speed away into the Unseen; take the gain and the treasure, and lament the pain no more."

15   Do you call aloud, and proclaim that you are King; yours is the grace of the answer, and yours is the knowledge of the question.

168

This time I am wholly involved in loverhood, this time I am wholly cut off from well-being.

I have plucked out my heart from myself, I am living with something else, I have burned up from root and stock reason and heart and thought.

O men, O men, manhood comes from me no more; the madman even does not meditate what I have meditated in my heart.

The unlucky madman has fled from my turbulence; I am commingled with death, I have flown into not-being.

5   Today my reason has become wholly disgusted with me; it desires to terrify me, thinking that I have no eyes.

Why indeed should I be afraid of it? I have put on a grimace for its sake. How should I be confused? But I am purposely so confounded.

I am quit of the bowl of the stars and the blood of the skies; I have licked many a bowl for the benefit of the beggarly-faced people.

For a good purpose I have remained in the prison of this world; what have I to do with prison? Whose property have I stolen?

In the body's prison I am drowned in blood, and of the tears of every stubborn one's eyes I have rubbed in the dust my blood-stained skirt.

10 Like an infant in the womb my nurture is of blood; ordinary men are born once, I have been born many times.

Examine me as much as you will, you will not recognize me, for I have become a hundred different manners from what you have seen me to be.

Enter my eye and behold me with my own sight, for I have chosen a dwelling place beyond all sight.

You are drunk, drunk and happy, I am drunk and happy, without a head; you are a lover with laughing lips, I am laughing without any mouth.

A strange bird am I, who of my own desire, without snare or catcher, have crept into the cage;

15 For the cage in the company of friends is sweeter than orchard and garden; to please the Josephs I have reposed in the well.

Do not bewail his blow, do not claim sickness; I have given a hundred sweet lives to purchase this calamity.

Like a silkworm at the cost of suffering you enter into satin and silk; give ear to a silkworm that has withered in the very garment.

You have withered in the tomb of the body; go before my Israfil saying, "For my sake blow on the trumpet, for I am weary of the tomb of the body."

No, no, like the well-tried falcon hood your eyes from yourself; I have put on brocade like a fine peacock.

ɔ   Bow your head to the physician saying, "Give me the antidote, for in this pleasant net I have swallowed many poisons."

Before the confectioner of the soul you will become sweet and sweet of soul, for from the confection of the soul I have waxed great as a sugarcane.

He will make your essence confection better than by giving a hundred confections; I have not heard the delight of the soul's confection save from his lips.

Be silent, for in speaking the confection falls out of the mouth; without speech a man catches a scent such as I have snuffed.

Every unripe grape is lamenting, "O Shams-i Tabrīzī, come, for on account of unripeness and lack of savour I groan within myself."

169

Yesterday my darling placed a golden crown on my head; however many blows you may strike, it will not fall from my head.

The cap-stitching king of eternity from his brows on my brows sets the nightcap of love, so of course it remains for ever.

And even if my head does not remain with the cap, I will become all head like the moon; for my pearl will appear brighter without casket and shell.

Here is my head, and there a heavy mace; strike, to make proof; and if this bone breaks, I am more full of marrow than intellect and soul.

5   That nut lacking pith which has chosen the husk—how shall it have perceived the relish of the almond-essence of my Prophet?

A sweetmeat full of his nuts, his sugar, and almonds sweetens my throat and lip, gives light to my eyes.

When you discover the pith, my son, and have learned to disregard the husk, when you have entered the quarter of Jesus, you will not any more say, "Where is my ass?"

My soul, how long will you complain? Give up one ass from

the herd; behold the stoutness of the rider, not my lean draught-horse.

Know that the stoutness of the lover derives from the stout-ness of his Beloved, for the pride of lovers arises from "I am God Most Great."

10   O sighing pains, do not say "Ah, ah," say "Allah"; speak not of the well, speak of the throne, O Joseph my soul-nourisher.

170

I was dead, I became alive; I was weeping, I became laughing; the power of love came, and I became everlasting power.

My eye is satiated, my soul is bold, I have the heart of a lion, I have become shining Venus.

He said, "You are not mad, you are not appropriate to this house"; I went and became mad, I became bound in shackles.

He said, "You are not intoxicated; go, for you belong not to this party"; I went and became intoxicated, I became overflowing with joy.

5   He said, "You are not slain, you are not drenched in joy"; before his life-giving face I became slain and cast down.

He said, "You are a clever little man, drunk with fancy and doubt"; I became a fool, I became straightened, I became plucked up out of all.

He said, "You have become a candle, the *qibla* of this assem-bly"; I am not of assembly, I am not candle, I have become scattered smoke.

He said, "You are shaikh and headman, you are leader and guide"; I am not a shaikh, I am not a leader, I have become slave to your command.

He said, "You have pinions and wings, I will not give you wings and pinions"; in desire for his pinions and wings I became wingless and impotent.

10   New fortune said to me, "Go not on the way, do not become pained, for out of grace and generosity I am now coming to you."

Old love said to me, "Do not move from my breast"; I said, "Yes, I will not, I am at rest and remain."

You are the fountain of the sun, I am the shadow of the willow; when You strike my head, I become low and melting.

My heart felt the glow of the soul, my heart opened and split, my heart wove a new satin, I became enemy of this ragged one.

The form of the soul at dawn swaggered insolently; I was a slave and an ass-driver, I became king and lord.

5 Your paper gives thanks for your limitless sugar, for it came into my embrace, and I dwelt with it.

My darkling earth gives thanks for my bent sky and sphere, for through its gaze and circling I became light-receiving.

The sphere of heaven gives thanks for king and kingdom and angel, for through his generosity and bounty I have become bright and bountiful.

The gnostic of God gives thanks that we have outraced all; above the seven layers I have become a shining star.

I was Venus, I became the moon, I became the two hundred-fold sky; I was Joseph, henceforth I have become the waxing Joseph.

10 Famous moon, I am yours, look upon me and yourself, for from the trace of your smile I have become a smiling rosegarden.

Move silently like a chessman, yourself all tongue, for through the face of the king of the world I have become happy and blissful.

171

Of these two thousand I's and we's I wonder, which one am I? Give ear to my babble, do not lay your hand on my mouth.

Since I have gone out of control, do not put glass on my path, for if you do I will stamp and break all that I find.

Because every moment my heart is confused with your fantasy, if you are joyous I am joyful, if you are sorrowing I am sorrowful.

You give bitterness and I become bitter, you give grace and I become all grace; with you it is pleasant, O my sugar-lipped, sweet-chinned idol.

5 You are the original—what person am I? A mirror in your

hand; whatever you show, that I become, I am a well-proved mirror.

You are like the cypress of the meadow, I am like your shadow; since I have become the shadow of the rose, I have pitched my tent beside the rose.

If without you I break off a rose, it will become a thorn in my hand; and if I am all thorn, through you I am all rose and jasmine.

Every moment I drain a bloody beaker of the blood of my heart; every instant I break my own pitcher against the saki's door.

Every second I reach out my hand towards the skirt of an idol, that he may scratch my cheek, that he may rend my shirt.

10   The grace of Ṣalāḥ-i Dil u Dīn shone in the midst of my heart; he is the heart's candle in the world; who am I? His bowl.

172

I saw a tree and a fire. A call came, "My darling!" That fire is calling me; am I Moses son of 'Imrān?

I entered the wilderness with affliction, and tasted manna and quails; for forty years like Moses I am wandering about this desert.

Ask not about ship and sea; come, look at these marvels—how that for so many years I have been sailing a ship in this dry land.

Come, soul! You are Moses, and this bodily form is your staff; when you pick me up I become a staff, when you cast me down I am a serpent.

5   You are Jesus and I am your bird; you made a bird out of clay; just as you breathe on me, even so I fly in the zenith.

I am the pillar of that mosque against which the Prophet leaned; when he leans against another, I moan from the pain of separation.

Lord of Lords and Formless Maker of forms, what form are You drawing over me? You know; I do not know.

Now I am stone, now iron; for a while I am all fire; now I am a balance without a weight, now I am both weight and balance.

For one time I pasture here, another they pasture on me; now I am a wolf, now a sheep, now the form of a shepherd.

o   The material body came as a token; how shall the token
remain for ever? Neither this remains nor that; He who is mine
knows that I am that.

173

I circumambulate with the pilgrims, I circle around the Be-
loved; I have not the character of dogs, I do not go around
carrion.

I am like a gardener; shovel laid on my neck, searching for a
cluster of dates I go around the thorns—

Not the kind of dates which, when you have eaten them, turn
to phlegm and make one bilious, but the kind that makes wings
to grow so that I circle like Ṭaiyār.

The world is a snake, and below it is a treasure very hidden; I
am on top of the treasure, and circle about it like the tail of a
snake.

I am not grieving for a grain, though about this house I circle
deep in thought like the heron.

I do not seek a house in the village, neither ox and fat herd,
but I am intoxicated with the Prince and circle seeking the
Prince.

I am the companion of Khiḍar and momently seek his ap-
proach, foot fast and circling, for like compasses I circle.

Do you not know that I am sick? For I am seeking Galen; do
you not see that I am crop-sick? For I circle the vintner.

Do you not know that I am Simurgh? For I fly around Qāf; do
you not know that I have caught the scent? For I circle about the
rosebower.

o   Count me not one of these men; recognize a phantom circling;
if I am not a phantom, O soul, why do I circle about the secrets?

Why do I not become still? I beat about this and that, for he
has unminded me and made me drunk, therefore I circle une-
venly.

You say to me, "Go not so hurriedly, for that shows disre-
spect"; I am ashamed of respect, therefore I circle shame.

I made bread my pretext, but I am intoxicated with the baker;
it is not about gold I circle, I circle about vision.

In every image which confronts me I behold the engraver; know that it is for love of Lailā that like Majnūn I circle.

15   In this palace of self-sacrificers in which is not contained even the head, I, bewildered, am pardonable if I circle without a turban.

I am not a flame-moth burning my wings and pinions, I am a moth of the King, for I circle about the lights.

Why do you bite my lips privily saying, "Be silent, do not speak"? Is it not your doing, your craft too that I circle about speech?

Come, Shams-i Tabrīzī, like twilight although you flee; like twilight in the track of the sun I circle about these lands.

174

I am not that luckless lover, to flee from the Beloved; I do not hold that dagger in my hand to flee from battle.

I am that plank with which the carpenter has much to do, I do not shrink from the axe or flee from the nails.

I am unselfed like a plank, I think not to oppose the axe; I am fit only for the flames if I flee from the carpenter.

I am as a worthless and cold stone if I do not journey oft to rubiness; I am as a dark and narrow cave if I flee from the Companion of the Cave.

5   I do not feel the kiss of the peach if I flee from leaflessness; I do not catch the scent of Tartary musk if I flee from the Tartar.

I am distressed with myself because I am not contained; it is meet, when the head is not contained, if I flee from the turban.

Many centuries are required for this fortune to emerge; where shall I find it again, if this time I flee?

It is not that I am sick and unmanly, that I shun the fair ones; it is not that my bowels are corrupt, that I flee from the vintner.

I am not mounted on a packsaddle to remain then in the arena; I am not a farmer of this village, to flee from the Prince.

10   I say, "My heart, have done"; my heart replies, "I am in the quarry of gold, why should I flee from the lavishing of riches?"

175

When the thunder and lightning laugh, I recite paeans of praise, I am full of light as the clear sky, I am circling around the moon.

My tongue is knotted like Moses because of the Pharaohs, for jealousy lest a Pharaoh should discover my proof.

Bind my hands if you find me in the encampment of a Pharaoh, for I am the Sultan's spy.

I am not a spy, I am not a scandal, I am one of the secrets of sanctity; let me go, since I am drunk, that I may let fly a vaunt.

5   From wine wind arises, for wine stirs up wind, especially the kind of wine through which I am distraught.

If a whiff of this wine were to reach all the world's ascetics, what a desolation then will appear, what shall I say? I know not.

Why speak of the wine? For if a whiff of those drunkards' breaths were to penetrate stone and marble, they would brag, "I am the Water of Life."

My being is a bachelor's apartment, and those drunkards are gathered together therein; my heart is distraught to know whether I am one of them—amazing!—or myself I am they.

Whether I am their congener, or whether I am other than they, I do not know; all I know is this, that I am in peace and well-being.

176

I went to the physician of the soul, I said, "Look at my hand. I am heartlorn and sick at once, both lover and intoxicated.

I have a hundred ailments—would that they were all one! With all these distempers I have reached the very end."

He said, "Were you not dead?" I said, "Yes, but when your scent came to me I leaped out of the grave."

That spiritual form, that orient divine, that Joseph of Canaan on whose account I wounded my hand,

5   Gently, gently came towards me and laid a hand on my heart.
He said, "Of what band are you?" I said, "Of this band."
When I brawled he gave me wine, and I drank; my pale cheek
glowed and I ceased to brawl.
Then I stripped off my clothes, I raged like a drunkard, I sat in
that drunkards' ring, on the right hand.
I drank a hundred jars, I roared a hundred ways, I scattered a
hundred glasses, I shattered a hundred pitchers.
Those folk worshipped the golden calf; I am a mangy calf, if I
do not worship Love.
10 Again the spiritual king is secretly calling me, he is drawing
me up royally from these depths.
I am foot-tied to you, O soul, I am intoxicated with you, my
soul, I am in your hand, my soul, whether I am arrow or
thumbstall.
If I am nimble, you make me so, if I am drunk you make me
so, if I am lowly you make me so, if I am in being, you make me
so.
You brought me into the circling sphere when you intoxicated
me with you; since now you have sealed the vat, I too have closed
my mouth.

177

Not for one single moment do I let hold of you, for you are
my whole concern, you are my whole affair.
I eat and enjoy your candy, I labour at your counselling; I am
a heart-wounded quarry, you are my heart-devouring lion.
You might say that my soul and your soul are one; I swear by
this one soul that I care not for other than you.
I am a bunch of herbs from the garden of your beauty, I am a
strand of your union's robe of honour.
5   Around you this world is thorn on the top of a wall; in the
hope of culling the rose of union it is a thorn that I scratch.
Since the thorn is like this, how must be your rosebower! O
you whose secrets have swallowed and borne away my secrets.
My soul, in the sky the sun is the moon's companion; I know
that you will not leave me in this assembly of strangers.

I went to a dervish and said, "May God befriend you!" You might say that through his blessing a king such as you became my friend.

I beheld the whole world to be a painting on the gates of a bath; you who have taken my turban away, likewise towards you I stretch my hand.

o Every congener bursts his chain to come to his congener; whose congener am I, who am held fast in this snare here?

Like a thief, my soul, you ever steal around me; I know what you are seeking, crafty sweetheart of mine.

My soul, you are hiding a candle under the cloak, you desire to set fire to my stook and rick.

O my rosebower and rosegarden, O cure of my sickness, O Joseph of my vision and lustre of my market,

You are circling round my heart, I am circling round your door; circling am I giddily in your hand like compasses.

5 In the gladness of your face if I tell the tale of woe, if then sorrow drinks my blood, by Allah, I deserve it.

To the beat of the tambourine of your decree all these creatures are dancing; without your melody does a single lute-string dance? I do not think so.

The voice of your tambourine is hidden, and this dance of the world is visible; hidden is that itch, wherever I scratch.

I will be silent out of jealousy, because from your sugarcane I am a cloud scattering sugar, it is only your candy that I rain.

I am in water, in earth, in fire, in air; these four are all around me, but I am not of these four.

20 Now I am Turk, now Hindu, now Rumi, now Zangi; it is of your engraving, my soul, that I believe or disbelieve.

Tabriz, my heart and soul are with Shams-i Ḥaqq here, even though in body I vex him no more.

178

I am a painter, a picture-maker, every moment I fashion an idol, then before you I melt away all the idols,

I raise up a hundred images and mingle them with spirit; when I see your image, I cast them in the fire.

You are the vintner's saki or the enemy of the sober, or the one who lays waste every house I build.

Over you the soul is poured forth, with you it is mingled; since the soul has the perfume of you, I will cherish the soul.

5   Every drop of blood that flows out of me says to your dust, "I am one in colour with your love, I am the playmate of your affection."

In the house of water and clay this heart without you is desolate; either enter the house, O soul, or I will abandon the house.

179

I am your disciple, for all that I am stupid and twisted of mouth, so that I may learn one smile from your smiling lip.

Fountain of learning, do you want me for a pupil? What device shall I invent to stitch myself to you?

At least I may descry through the crack of the door the lightning of your cheek; from that fire of the portico I will kindle a hundred candles.

One instant you rob me of my load on the way, saying, "I am the tithe-collector"; one instant you go before me, meaning, "I am the guide."

5   Now you drive me to sin, now towards repentance; twist my head and my tail, for I am a compressed *hamza*.

In sin and in penitence, like a fish on the pan, this side and that side I am burning on the pan.

On your pan I am turning this way and that; in the darkness of night, with you I am brighter than day.

Enough, I am all diversified in craft and thought; for one instant like turquoise, for one instant like Pīrūz.

180

Once again, once again I have escaped from my chains, I have burst out of these bonds and this trap which seizes the infirm.

Heaven, the bent old man full of wizardry and deceit—by virtue of your youthful fortune I have escaped from this old man.

Night and day I ran, I broke away from night and day; ask of this sphere how like an arrow I sped.

Why should I fear sorrow? For I am the comrade of death. Why should I fear the general? For I have escaped from the prince.

Reason bore me down with anxiety for forty years; sixty-two has made me quarry, and I have escaped from devising.

All creatures have been made deaf or blind by predestination; I have escaped from the deaf and blind of predestination, and from predestination.

Outwardly skin, inwardly stone, the fruit is a prisoner; like a fig, I have escaped from that skin and that stone.

Delay causes mischief, and haste is of the devil; my heart has escaped from haste, and I have escaped from delay.

In the first place blood was the food, in the end blood became milk; when the teeth of reason sprouted, I escaped from that milk;

o   I ran after bread, a loaf or two, by imposture; God gave me a food, so that I escaped from imposture.

Be silent, be silent, speak no more in detail; I will speak of the interpretation, I have escaped from the stench of garlic.

181

Like a mirror my soul displays secrets; I am able not to speak, but I am unable not to know.

I have become a fugitive from the body, fearful as to the spirit; I swear I know not—I belong neither to this nor to that.

Seeker, to catch a scent is the condition of dying; look not upon me as living, for I am not so.

Look not on my crookedness, but behold this straight word; my talk is an arrow, and I am as a bow.

This gourdlike head on top of me, and this dervish habit of my body—whom am I like, whom am I like in this market of the world?

Then this gourd on my head, full of liquor—I keep it upside down, yet I let not a drop trickle from it.

And even if I do let trickle, do you behold the power of God, that in exchange for that drop I gather pearls from the sea.

My eyes like a cloud gather pearls from that sea; this cloud of my spirit rises to the heaven of fidelity.

I rain in the presence of Shams al-Ḥaqq-i Tabrīz, that lilies may grow in the form of my tongue.

182

Saki, my spirit is moving in the track of love, but because of your weariness my tongue is tied.

Like an arrow I am flying towards your joyous company; beloved, do not break my bow with cruelties.

Like a tent I remain standing before you on one foot; beloved, bring me into your tabernacle and seat me there.

Ho, lay that flagon's lip on my dry lip, then hear the veritable magic from my mouth;

5   Hear the story of Babylon and the tale of Vā'il, for by way of meditation I travel the world.

Excuse me if my turbulence goes beyond bounds, since love grants me security not for a single moment.

When you are weary, I am weary of your weariness; when you wash your hands of me, I bite my fingers.

On the night when you dispense light like the moon until daybreak, in your wake I am running like a star;

On the day when you put up your head from the east like the sun, like the sun I am altogether spirit.

10   But on the day when like the spirit you are hidden from my eyes, like the heart of a bird I am fluttering with anxiety.

On the day when your light shines through my window, in my apartment I dance for joy like a mote.

Rational soul, be silent and depart into hiding like the thought, so that he who thinks of causes only may not find my track.

183

I am the slave who set the master free, I am the one who taught the teacher.

I am that soul which was born of the world yesterday, and yet erected the ancient world.

I am the wax whose claim is this, that it was I who made steel steel.

I have painted with surmeh many a sightless one, I have taught many a one without intelligence.

I am the black cloud in the night of grief who gladdened the day of festival.

I am the amazing earth who out of the fire of love filled with air the brain of the sky.

In joy that king slept not last night, because I the slave remembered him.

It is not to blame, since you intoxicated me, if I am scandalous and wrought injustice.

Silence, for the mirror is rusting over; when I blew upon it, it protested against me.

184

I made a journey, I ran to every city, no man I saw with your grace and beauty.

I returned from banishment and exile, once more I attained this felicity.

Since I became far from the garden of your countenance, I saw no rose, I plucked not one fruit.

Since by bad luck I fell far from you, I have endured trouble from every unlucky one.

What shall I say? I was utterly dead without you; God has created me anew once more.

Amazing! Would you say that I have beheld your face? Would you say that I have heard your voice?

Suffer me to kiss your hand and foot; give festively, for today is festival.

Joseph of Egypt, I have brought you as a present such a bright mirror.

185

How close your soul is to my soul! For whatever thing you are thinking, I know.

I have a token even closer than this; come close, and behold my token.

In dervish guise you come into the midst; do not jest and say, "I am in the midst."

I am like the column amidst your house; I am like a waterspout hanging down from your roof.

5   I am a sharer of your secrets on the day of mustering and resurrection, I am not a passing host like worldly friends.

In your banquet I go round like the wine, in time of your battle I go before you like a lance.

If like lightning I make a trade of dying, like the lightning of your beauty I am without a tongue.

Always I am joyful; it makes no difference whether I yield my soul, or seize a soul.

If I give you my soul, it will be good trade, for in exchange for a soul you will give me a hundred worlds.

10   In this house thousands and more are dead; there you are seated saying, "Behold my household!"

A handful of dust says, "I was once a tress"; another says, "I am a bone."

You become bewildered; then suddenly Love comes saying, "I will deliver you this very instant from yourself."

Silence, Khusrau, speak no more of Shīrīn; my mouth is burning with sweetness.

186

Out of all the world I choose you alone; do you deem it right for me to sit sorrowful?

My heart is like a pen in your hand; through you it is, whether
I am glad or grieve.

What shall I be other than what you wish? What shall I see
except what you show?

Now you cause thorns to grow from me, now roses; now I
smell roses, now I pluck thorns.

5 Since you keep me so, I am so—since you wish me so, I am so.

In that vat where you dispense dye to the heart, what should I
be? What my love and hate?

You were the first, and you will be the last; do you make my
last better than my first.

When you are hidden, I am of the infidels; when you appear, I
am of the faithful.

What do I possess other than the thing you have given? What
are you searching for in my pocket and sleeve?

187

Come, for today we are the quarry of the King, we have no
need for self and the world.

Come, for today like Moses son of 'Imrān we will lift up dust
from the sea.

All night we were fallen like staves; now that day has come
we are restless as serpents.

Having circumambulated round our own breast, we bring out
of the soul's pocket the White Hand.

5 By that power whereby a serpent became a staff, every night
we are like a staff, daily a serpent;

For arrogant Pharaoh we are serpents, for Moses we are staves
and obedient.

By zeal we shed the blood of Nimrods; do not regard the fact
that we are slender as gnats.

We will exceed over lions and elephants, though in the hand
of that Lion we are helpless.

Though like camels we are crooked of nature, like camels we
travel smoothly towards the Kaaba.

10 We will not attach our hearts to a two-days' fortune, for we
are successful in everlasting fortune.

Like sun and moon we are near and far, like love and the heart we are hidden and patent.

For the sake of blood-lapping, blood-devouring Love we are as blood in the platter of Love's dogs.

As fish in the time of silence we are silent, in the time of speech we are the dustless moon.

188

I was intent on seeking a stratagem, that that moon-faced one might set his face on mine.

I said, "I have one word in my mind; come forward, that I may speak it in your ear.

Last night, dear soul, I saw a dream, and I desire to seek from you its interpretation.

I have none intimate with this dream but you; do you listen, my king whose habit is to conceal."

5   He moved his head and laughed—that head which knows me hair by hair—

As if to say, "You are hatching a trick to play on me, for I am the mirror of every hue and scent."

I am as a plaything in his hands, for I am the picture drawn by his gold-stitching needle.

Not lifeless shall be the image which he has made; I am his least image, I am therefore in ecstasy.

189

I departed, ridding the world of the trouble of my presence, I escaped from anguish with my life;

I bade farewell to my companions, I transported my soul to the signless world.

I went forth from this house of six doors, gaily I carried my baggage to placelessness.

When I beheld the master of the hunt of the Unseen I flew like an arrow, carrying my bow;

5   When the polo-stick of death approached me, I carried off
from the midst the ball of felicity.

A marvellous moon shone through my window; I went to the
roof, carrying a ladder.

The roof of heaven which is the assembly-place of souls, was
fairer than I had ever imagined.

Since my rose-branch had become withered, I carried it back
again to the garden and rosebower.

As there was no purchaser for my coin, I carried it quickly to
the source of the source of the mine;

10   From these counterfeiters I carried also as a present a filing of
the soul to the goldsmith.

In the Unseen the boundless world I saw; to that bound I
transported my tent.

Do not weep for me, for I am happy because of this journey,
inasmuch as I have travelled the road to the realm of paradise.

Write this saying upon my tomb, that I have come safely out
of trial and tribulation.

Sleep sweetly, body, in this earth, for I have carried your
message up to heaven.

15   Bind up my chin, for I have carried all lamentations to the
Creator of lamentation.

Speak no more the grief of your heart, for I have carried your
heart to the presence of Him who knows all secrets.

190

We are dancing like motes, we obey the command of your sun.
Every dawn out of Love's east like the sun we rise.

We thresh about in dry and wet, we become not dry, nor turn
wet.

We have heard brasses making much lament, "O light, shine,
that we may become gold."

5   For the sake of their need and anguish we rise to the spheres
and the stars.

We come as amber for a necklace from the silver-bosomed
Beloved.

We have beaten our dervish frock, to emerge from that to a
gown of Shushtar.

We are the drainers of pure wine on the path of poverty, we are intoxicated with the red wine.

If they impose on us the world's poison, we come as sugar out of our inward parts.

10 On the day when brave men flee, we come as Sanjar in the thick of the battle;

We make wine of the foeman's blood, then we drain it and come like daggers.

We are the ring of drunken lovers, every day we come as a ring on the door.

He wrote the sign-manual of security for us; how should we come to the rattle of mere death?

In the supernal kingdom and placelessness we come on the steed of the green sphere.

15 We went into hiding from the world of the flesh, we come more manifest in the world of Love.

In the body the soul has become pure; we become bodiless and come yet purer.

Shams-i Tabrīz is the soul of the soul; we come shoulder to shoulder in the house of eternity.

191

Last night I vowed anew, I swore an oath by your life,

That I would never remove my eyes from your face; if You smite with the sword, I will not turn from You.

I will not seek the cure from any other, because my pain is of separation from You.

If You should cast me into the fire, I am no true man if I utter a sigh.

5 I rose from your path like dust; now I return to the dust of your path.

192

If I do not express in speech your elegance, I have your love within my breast.

If I smell a rose without your love, forthwith burn me like a thorn.

If I am silent as a fish, yet I am restless as the waves and the sea.

You who have set a seal on my lips, draw my toggle towards You.

5   What is your design? What should I know? I only know that I am in this train.

I chew the cud of grief for you like a camel, like a raging camel I bring up foam.

Though I keep hidden and do not speak, in the presence of Love I am manifest.

I am like a seed under the soil, I am waiting upon the signal of spring,

That without my own breath I may breathe sweetly, that without my own head I may scratch a head.

193

On the day when you pass over my grave, bring to mind this terror and confusion of mine;

Fill full of light that bottom of the tomb, O eye and lamp of my light,

That in the tomb this patient body of mine may prostrate to you in gratitude.

Harvest of roses, pass me not in haste, make me happy a moment with that perfume;

5   And when you pass by, do not suppose that I am far from your window and portico.

If the stones of the tomb have blocked my way, I am unwearying on the path of fantasy.

Though I should have a hundred winding-sheets of satin, I am naked without the vestment of your form.

I will emerge into the hall of your palace, in breaking a hole in the wall perchance I am like an ant.

I am your ant, you are Solomon; not for one moment leave me without your presence.

10   I have fallen silent; do you speak the rest, for I am shunning henceforth my own speaking and listening.

Shams-i Tabrīz, do you invite me, since your invitation is my
blast of the trumpet.

194

We are living by the light of Majesty, we are strangers and
exceeding familiar.

The carnal soul is like a wolf, but in our secret heart we are
superior to Joseph of Egypt.

The moon repents of his conceit when we display to him our
face;

The feathers and pinions of the sun consume when we open
our feathers and pinions.

5   This form of man is a veil; we are the *qibla* of all prostra-
tions.

Regard that breath, do not see the Adam in us, that we may
transport your soul with grace.

Iblis looked with a separate regard, he supposed that we are
apart from God.

Shams-i Tabrīz himself is the pretext; it is we who are in the
beauty of grace, we.

For the sake of a veil say to men, "He is the noble king and we
are beggars."

10   What have we to do with kingship and beggary? We are
happy because we are worthy of the king.

We are effaced in the beauty of Shams-i Tabrīz; in that
effacement neither he is, nor are we.

195

O world of water and clay, since I knew you I have known a
myriad tribulations and pains.

You are the pasturage of asses, not the abode of Jesus; why
have I known this pasturage of asses?

You first spread the table, then gave me sweet water; you
bound me hand and foot, so that I knew hand and foot.

Why should you not bind hand and foot, seeing God called
you a cradle?

5   Like a tree I lift up my hands from the earth in desire for that
One from whom I knew desire.

"O cluster, how is it that in childhood you become like a
perfect old man?" Answer came, "I escaped from youthful pas-
sion when I knew the zephyr."

The branch goes upwards because it came from above; I
hasten towards my origin, because I know my origin.

How long shall I speak of "below" and "above"? Placelessness
is my origin, I am not of place, for I know whence place comes.

No, be silent, depart into nonexistence, become naught in
nonexistence; behold, how I know things from no-things!

196

Since my sun and star arose higher than form, I am happier to
go from realities into realities.

I have become lost in realities—so it is sweeter; I will not
return towards form, I will not look upon the two worlds.

I am melting in meanings till I become of one colour with
Him, for meaning is as water and I am as sugar.

No man's heart wearies of the life of his own soul; naturally in
view of this reality I will not recall form.

5   I stroll from garden to garden with the spiritual ones, graceful
as a red rose and fresh as a nenuphar am I.

I am as a wave to the body's boat, I break it plank by plank; I
smash myself when I am anchor to myself.

And if out of hardness of heart I am slack in my affairs, swiftly
out of the sea surge my flames of fire.

I am laughing happily as gold amidst his fire, because if I
emerge from the fire I congeal as gold.

From an incantation like a snake I have put down my head on
his line—brother, what will fall on my head from his line?

10   I was weary of form, I came towards attributes; each attribute
said, "Enter here, for I am the green sea."

Shams-i Tabrīz, I have a realm like Alexander; consequently
out of grace I am army-leader towards the armies of meaning.

197

Give me that last night's wine, for I am intoxicated by your potion; Ḥātim of the world, give into my hand a huge cup.

Saki of true men, turn not your face from me for one moment; do not break my heart, else I shall break cup and glass.

A cup was in my hand, I flung it down and broke it; I wounded the soles of a hundred naked feet with that glass.

You are a glass-worshipper because your liquor is from glass; my wine is not of must, so why should I worship glass?

5   Drink, my heart, the spiritual wine, and sleep secure and free of care; for I have beheaded anguish, I have escaped from sorrow and anguish.

My heart has gone up, my body has gone down; where am I, the helpless one? I am neither above nor below.

What a fine hanging apple am I, who cannot endure without your stone! How should I endure without *balā* if I am drunk with *alast?*

Ask of me, what a treasure this love is and what it holds; ask concerning me also of him, that he may say who I am.

Why do you hang about the riverbank? Leap from the river, if you are a true man; leap from the river and seek for me, for I have leaped from the river.

10   If you remain, we remain, and if you go, we depart; when you ate I ate, when you sat I sat.

I am that drunken drummer who went drunk into the arena, I tied my drum like a flag to the top of my lance.

What a happy and unselfed king you are! Ho, silent as a fish —since I have escaped from being, why do you draw me back to being?

198

I am that lover of your love who have no occupation but this, for I have nothing but disapproval for him who is not a lover.

I seek no heart but yours, I hurry only towards you; I do not smell the roses of every garden, I have no heed for every thorn.

In you I have put my faith, my heart has become Mussulman; my heart said to you, "Darling, I have no beloved like you."

Since you are my eye and tongue, I do not see two, I do not recite two, I acknowledge none but the one darling that is you.

Since I drink of your honey, why should I sell vinegar? Why should I labour for my daily bread? It is not the case that I do not possess an ample allowance.

I eat to my fill at this table of the Sultan's sugarcakes, not as a guest of Satan; I have no appetite for lunch.

I will not grieve, I will not grieve, I will not boast of asceticism; if you think I have not abundant gold, behold my gold-pale cheeks.

The Khusrau of the heart grieves only for Shīrīn; with what heart should I grieve? After all, I have not a grieved heart.

I would explain for all, both fearful and secure alike; but I have not the heart to speak of inward words.

You who are unbranded by madness, tell me now, how are you? For I have no further traces of how and after what manner.

Since from Tabriz has come the moon of Shams al-Ḥaqq u Dīn to me, I have no care for the moon of the dormitory of the commander.

199

If I am hand-clapping, I belong not to the clappers; I am neither of this nor of that, I am of that mighty city.

I am not for fluting and gambling, I am not for wine and liquor, I am neither leaven nor crop-sickness, I am neither like this nor like that.

If I am drunk and dissolute, I am not drunk with wine like you; I am not of earth nor of water, I am not of the people of time.

The mind of the son of Adam—what knowledge has it of this utterance? For I am hidden by two hundred veils from the world entire.

Hear not these words as from me, nor from this clear thought, for I neither receive nor seize this outward and inward.

Though your face is beautiful, the cage of your soul is of wood; run away from me or you will burn, for my tongue is a flame.

I am not of scent nor colour, I am not of fame nor shame; beware of my poplar arrow, for God is my bow.

I seize not raw wine, nor borrow from anyone, I seize neither breath nor snare, O my youthful fortune.

I am as the rosebower of paradise, I am the joy-garden of the world, for my spirit is flowing through the spirits of all men.

10   The sugarbed of your phantom brings rose-sugar to me; in the garden of realities I scatter the rose of a hundred petals.

When I enter the rose-showering garden of union with you, make me sit down, for I am a target for your brand.

Love, what a mate you are, how strange, how marvellous! When you seized my mouth, my expression went inwards.

When my soul reaches Tabriz, to come to Shams al-Ḥaqq u Dīn, I will bring to an end all the secrets of speech.

200

There is a passion in my head that I have no inclination for mankind, this passion makes me so that I am unaware of myself.

The king of love bestows every moment two thousand kingdoms; I desire nothing from him save his beauty.

The girdle and cap of his love are enough for me in both worlds; what matter if my cap falls? What care if I have no girdle?

One morning his love transported my wounded heart to a place where I transcended day and night, and have no knowledge of dawn.

5   A journey befell my soul to the kingdom of realities, such that the sky and the moon say, "I have no such journey."

Through separation if my soul scatters pearls from my eyes, think not that I have not a heart full of pearls from him.

What sugar-seller have I to sell sugar to me! Never on any day he said, "Go, for I have no sugar."

I would have shown a token of his beauty, but the two worlds would be confounded; I have no inclination for such clamour and riot.

Tabriz, I have sworn that after Shams-i Dīn comes I will in gratitude lay down this head, for I have nothing but a head.

Bibliography

Badī al-Zamān Furūzānfar. *Kullīyāt-i Shams.* 8 vols. Tehran, 1336–45 (1957–66). Critical edition of the collected odes, quatrains, and other poems of Rūmī, with glossary and notes.

————. *Zindagānī-yi Maulānā Jalāl al-Dīn Muhammad.* 2d ed. Tehran, 1333 (1954). Biography of Rūmī.

R. A. Nicholson. *Selected Poems from the Dīvāni Shamsi Tabrīz.* Cambridge: At the University Press, 1898. Introduction, selected texts, translations, and notes.

————. *The Mathnawī of Jalāu'ddīn Rūmī.* 8 vols. London: Luzac & Co., 1925–40. Critical edition, translation, and commentary on Rūmī's mystical epic.

————. *Rūmī, Poet and Mystic.* London: George Allen & Unwin, 1950. Introduction and select translations.

A. J. Arberry. *The Rubā'īyāt of Jalāl al-Dīn Rūmī.* London, 1949. Introduction and verse translations.

————. *Discourses of Rumi.* London: John Murray, 1961. Annotated translation of the *Fīhi mā fīhi*, Rumi's occasional conversations.

Aflākī. *Manāqib al-'ārifīn.* 2 vols. Ankara, 1959–61. Biographies of Rumi and his circle, edited by Tahsin Yazıcı.

Afzal Iqbal. *The Life and Thought of Rumi.* Lahore, 1957.

Entries on Rumi in the standard histories of Persian literature may also be consulted, as well as works on Sufism and Persian mysticism as listed in the encyclopedias.

Notes

Abbreviations

CB = Chester Beatty manuscript Persian 116
Dozy = R. Dozy, *Supplément aux dictionnaires arabes* (Leiden, Paris, 1927)
E.I. = *Encyclopaedia of Islam* (London, 1908–34; new edition [2] London, 1960—)
F = edition of Badī' al-Zamān Furūzānfar (see Bibliography)
Lane = E. W. Lane, *An Arabic-English Lexicon* (London, 1863–85)
Math = *Mathnawī* of Rūmī (see Bibliography)
N = selection by R. A. Nicholson (see Bibliography)
Yāqūt = *Mu 'jam al-buldān* (Cairo, 1906)

Note: The numbers introducing each note refer to verses, not lines.

I

F 3
3. "Dark thoughts": doubts of God's benevolence, as in Koran 33:10. "Such drawing, such tasting": cf. *Math.* I:887, "This attraction (by which God draws the soul towards Himself) comes from the same quarter whence came that savour (spiritual delight experienced in and after prayer)."
5. CB reads *az balā* for *mar turā*, which it notes as a variant.
6. It is God who puts fear into the hearts of sinners to induce them to repent; see Koran 17:61.
8. "The light of the form of Muṣṭafā": the *nūr-i Muḥammadī*, equivalent to Universal Reason, which has inspired all the prophets and saints, see Nicholson on *Math.* II:909 and Massignon in *E.I.* III:961.
11. The story of Shu'aib, prophet to the Midianites, is told in Koran 7:83–91, 11:85–98.
15. This verse is cited by Aflākī, *Manāqib al-'ārifīn* 397. The source of the story of Shu'aib weeping was evidently 'Aṭṭār, *Ilāhī-nāma* 6140–56.
21. Bā Yazīd (Abū Yazīd-i Bisṭāmī), the famous mystic of Khorasan (d. 261/874 or 264/877), is the hero of many spiritual anecdotes; see Ritter in *E.I.*[2] I:162–63. The point of this anecdote is the pun between *kharbanda* (ass-driver) and *banda-yi Khudā* (slave of God).

167

2

F 14
4. For Moses striking the Red Sea with his staff, see Koran 20:19.
5. CB reads *bāda* (wine) for *bād* (wind).
8. CB reads *ravam* (I go) for *ravī* (you go). The CB reading *hastīm* (being) is perhaps superior to *mastīm* (drunkenness).
9. For Moses on Mount Sinai, see Koran 9:138–39.
11. CB reads *bāda* for *bād*, yielding the perhaps superior meaning, "what wine have you drunk?"

3

F 19
1. "Like the spirit of Muṣṭafā": a reference to the famous *mi'rāj* (Ascension) of Muhammad. The orthodox view was that his ascension was bodily, but Rūmī is attracted by the double meaning of *ravān* ("departing" and "spirit").
2. "Confused": lit. "Latticed."
3. The posture of prostration in prayer symbolizes the subjection of reason to spirit.

4

F 26
3. Man is composed of water and clay. Rūmī puns on *durd* (dregs) and *dard* (pains).
9. Rūmī puns on *charā* (graze) and *chirā* (why).

5

F 34
8. Many of Rūmī's poems end with a command to silence, to conceal the *mysterium tremendum* of the ineffable experience of the Divine. God is called *al-Sattār* because of His clemency; He veils the faults of men.

6

F 45
2. Khiḍar (Khaḍir, Khiḍr) was the mysterious guide who led Alexander (Dhu'l-Qarnain) to the Fountain of Immortality, and is the associate of mystics; see Wensinck in *E.I.* II:861–65.

3. Rūmī puns on *chashma* (fountain) and *chashm* (eye); intoxication is the term poets use to describe the languorous eye of the beautiful beloved.
5. Selfhood must be abandoned if the mystic would attain to union with the Beloved.
6. Duality is the fatal impediment to unity.
8. For Moses and the Burning Bush, see Koran 20:12.
16. Rūmī refers to the Table sent down by God in response to Jesus, see Koran 5:114–15. Onions and chives were preferred to the heavenly ambrosia by the unbelieving Jews.
17. There is a play on *shūr* (riot) and *shūrbā* (broth).
18. A pun on *zabāna* (flame) and *zabān* (tongue).

7

F 58
1. "The fair one of Canaan": Joseph (here as often symbol for the Divine Beauty), in wonderment at whose loveliness the women of Egypt cut their hands; see Koran 12:31.
3. A play on *kūhī* (a mountain) and *kāhī* (a straw).
6. The hoopoe was the Queen of Sheba's messenger to Solomon, see Koran 27:21–30.
7. Solomon was given knowledge of the speech of the birds, see Koran 27:16. Rūmī doubtless knew 'Aṭṭār's mystical epic the *Manṭiq al-ṭair*.
8. Solomon had dominion over the winds, see *E.I.* IV:520.

8

F 64
2. Vāmiq and 'Adhrā were lovers famed in Persian legend; their romance was the subject of a lost epic by 'Unṣurī. The poet puns (pardon) on the name of 'Adhrā.
6. When Abraham was cast by Nimrod's orders into the flames, the fire was miraculously changed into roses; see Koran 21:69 and Nicholson on *Math.* I:547.
9. Kauthar is a river in paradise, Riḍwān the angel-gardener who holds the key to the heavenly gate.
11. The legendary 'Anqā nests in the mountain of Qāf on the edge of the world.
12. "Neither of the east nor of the west": see Koran 24:35.

9

F 69
6. "Who brings the dead to life": see Koran 7:55.

10

F 80
9. For Goha the fool and jester, see Nicholson on *Math.* II:3116.
For Bū Bakr the Lutanist, see Nicholson on *Math.* II:1573.

11

F 84

12

F 100
3. "The bowl has fallen again from the roof": "a metaphor conveying the idea of divulgation, exposure, and notoriety" (Nicholson on *Math.* II:2061).
5. In sleep the soul is liberated from the body; see Nicholson on *Math.* I:400.
7. The miracle of Moses' staff, see Koran 7:110–14, 20:68–69.

13

F 110
2. A play on the two meanings of *chang* (clutches, harp).

14

F 115
1. A play on the two meanings of *ravān.*
3. Conventional images of human (material) beauty.
6. A play on the two meanings of *miyān* (midst, waist).
11. "The sugar-sprinkler": the divine source of all sweetness and joy.
13. I.e. do not expose our romance to idle gossip.

15

F 122
9. God is the All-rich, needing nothing in His perfection: Koran 2:265, etc.
10. The reference is to Koran 19:25.

16

F 132
1. The sufferings of love lead to incomparable joy.
2. Love knows to transcend the physical universe of Reason.
4. The reference is to Ḥallāj, the martyr-mystic, executed in 309/922.
6. "The courtyard": perhaps "annihilation (fanā)."

17

F 143, N 3
5. This verse is cited by Aflākī, Manāqib 743, with the readings jān (soul) for dil (heart), and girya-sh ("its weeping," so Nicholson also) for gardish ("turning about," perhaps rather, "its dust," i.e. distress).
7. The eye of the Beloved is intoxicating as well as intoxicated. Nicholson reads and translates differently.

18

F 163
1. This poem was probably composed after Shams al-Dīn's first disappearance from Konya.
7. The rubies of Yemen were proverbial for excellence.

19

F 166, N 5
8. Muslim brides have henna painted on their hands in patterns.
11. The four elements are earth, air, fire and water.

20

F 171
1. Even inanimate nature is moved to ecstasy, like the whirling dervishes, by the epiphany of Divine Beauty.
6. Mirrors were made of steel, and became rusty with age.
8. Venus is the harpist leading the heavenly choir, cf. 19 line 6.

After this line CB adds a ninth: "O image of his beauty, drive slowly, wait for the lame travellers."

21

F 181

Aflākī, *Manāqib* 370–1, relates as follows the circumstances under which this poem was composed. "One day Shaikh Ṣadr al-Dīn (Qōnawī) and Qāḍī Sirāj al-Dīn with other ulema and gnostics had gone out to visit the congregational mosque of Marām, and the Maulānā (Rūmī) also graced the gathering. After a while he rose up and coming to a mill, remained there a long time, so that the company waited for him beyond measure. Then the Shaikh and Qāḍī Sirāj al-Dīn came to look for him at the mill. They saw that the Maulānā was circling about the mill; said he, 'By the right of His right, this mill-stone is saying, "Glorious and Holy is He!"' The Shaikh related: 'I and Qāḍī Sirāj al-Dīn that very moment heard proceeding from that mill-stone the sound, 'Glorious and Holy is He!' Then he commenced this poem."

22

F 188
2. Cf. *Math.* II:2324: "Intellect shows itself in many guises, but like the peri is leagues removed from them." See Nicholson's note *ad loc.;* the peri (= jinn) can assume at will various alien forms. For the comparison of the heart to a pond fed by streams, see Nicholson on *Math.* I:2710–14.
4. "Superintendence": reading with CB, *ishrāf* for *ishrāq.*
5. For the five inward senses, see Nicholson on *Math.* I:3576.
7. "Burnishing": i.e. making the mirror the mind clear.
8. Too much conceit of freedom of action leads to disaster.

23

F 196
4. A play on *khazān* (autumn) and *khīzān* (rising).
8. A play on the two meanings of *ravān.*
10. "The treasury": the roses blooming to entrance the nightingales.

24

F 207, N 6
Nicholson's text of this poem differs in numerous places.

5. "The seven oft-repeated verses": Sura 1 of the Koran, to be recited in every prayer.
12. As God said to Moses on Sinai, see Koran 7:139.
13. Rūmī has realized the Muslim Unity of God, the Christian Trinity, and the Magian Duality.

25

F 211
11. "Puckered": reading with CB *turunjīda*, punning on *turunj*.
14. This verse is in Arabic in the original.

26

F 213, N 1
Nicholson's text exhibits numerous variants.
3. "That madman": Majnūn (Qais), the poet-lover of Lailā in the famous Bedouin romance. There is a wordplay between *shaid* (wile) and *shaidā* (wild).
5. "The spider": probably the one which spun a web hiding the entrance to the cave in which Muhammad took refuge in his flight from Mecca. "My Lord the Most High": cf. Koran 79:24.
6. "He carried His servant by night": Koran 17:1, the allusion to Muhammad's *mi'rāj*.
7. Vīsa and Rāmīn, Vāmiq and 'Adhrā were lovers famed in Persian legend and epopee.

27

F 221
6. Cf. Koran 73:17.

28

F 232
The circumstances of the composition of this poem (and others) are related at length by Aflākī, *Manāqib* 179–82. (F's text differs considerably from the Ankara edition.) The date 656/125 is given.
7. Ghūṭa was the region surrounding Damascus, abounding in trees and rivers: Yāqūt VI:314. Nairab was a village near Damascus set about with gardens: Yāqūt VIII:355.
14. Rūmī uses medical images.

16. The Cadi of Kāb (on whose authority Aflākī related the anecdote) had come to pay homage to Rūmī.

19. This and the verse following are in Arabic.

29

F 239, N 2

6. See note on 7 line 6.

10. Nicholson reads *Kaivān* (Saturn) for *aivān* (portico), and then inserts two extra couplets.

12. Ṣalāḥ al-Dīn Zarkūb, who died *c.* 659/1261, was Rūmī's *pīr* after Shams al-Dīn vanished; he is here hailed as an embodiment of the Spirit of Muhammad, the Perfect Man.

30

F 246

3. For Ḥallāj, see note on 16 line 4. The "people of purity" are the saintly Sufis.

31

F 250

3. "Splitter of Dawn": Koran 6:96. "Lord of the Daybreak": Koran 113:1.

4. See the story told in *Math.* I:3056–64.

11. Mount Ḥirā: the hill outside Mecca to which Muhammad withdrew for meditation.

32

F 260

5. Man is the *khalīfa* of God in the world: Koran 2:28.

8. The notion of congenerity is a favourite theme with Rūmī, see *Math.* I:745, IV:2664, VI:1175, etc.

33

F 294

2. For Ilyās (Elias) and his association in Muslim legend with Khiḍar (Khaḍir), see Wesinck in *E.I.* II:470–71.

5. "Water of the face" is a metaphor for honour, self-respect. The poverty here mentioned is of course spiritual self-surrender.
6. "The water": of Divine Grace, the Sea of the Soul.
13. See note on 15, line 10.
15. I.e. relapse into silence.

34

F 304
The circumstances under which this poem was composed are related in Aflākī, Manāqib 165–7. Comparison with the opening verses of the Mathnavi is relevant.
3. "To God": cf. Koran 3:12.
8. For the theme, see Math. III:3901, IV:3637 and cf. Koran 23:13.
10. See Koran 31:21.
12. The language of Divine Love is international.
15. "Speech": the Logos mediating between God and man.
20. Koran 47:4. The only course with deniers of spiritual values is, not tenderness, but outright rejection.

35

F 310, N 7
See Aflākī, Manāqib 453, 569. For a verse translation, see Nicholson, Rūmī, Poet and Mystic, p. 161.

36

F 314
4. Cf. Omar Khayyám—Fitzgerald's "Two-and-seventy jarring sects."
8. A pun on the two meanings of qaḍā (fate, fulfilment).

37

F 321

38

F 322
5. A pun on gul (rose) and kull (all). Many passages of the Koran open with the word "say."

6. The *Fātiḥa* is the first Sura of the Koran.

11. "I am cooking you": CB reads *pazānamat* for *parānamat*.

39

F 330

See Aflākī, *Manāqib* 161, on Rūmī preaching to dogs at the cross-roads.

5. As on the Resurrection Day the scrolls of men's deeds will flutter over their heads.

40

F 332, N 15

6. After this CB adds an extra couplet: "This is the house of the soul, it is the same place as the soul is, it is neither below nor above nor the six directions, for it is the middle."

12. See note on 7 line 1.

14. "It is inauspicious": perhaps rather, "Become intoxicated."

18. A play on *zabān* (tongue) and *zabāna* (flame).

41

F 341

8. Junaid (d. 298/910) was the chief of the Sufis of Baghdad. For Bā Yazīd, see note on 1, line 21.

42

F 359

7. The idea seems to be that the moon's occultation is during union with the sun; the terms "united" and "separation" belong to the technical vocabulary of Sufism.

43

F 364

1. This and the following two couplets are a quotation from Sanā'ī, see his *Dīvān* (ed. Riḍavī) 589.

5. The Night of Power (see Koran 97:1) was the night (of Ramaḍān) on which the Koran was first revealed; see Nicholson on *Math.* II:2935.

44

F 376
3. The reference is to Koran 12:20. Th springtide of mystical joy is seen as Joseph delivered out of the well of the winter of exclusion.

45

F 381
4. The simurgh (the fabulous griffin) symbolizes the mystic adept and leader, as in 'Aṭṭar's *Manṭiq al-ṭair*.

46

F 393
3. Cf. Koran 24:39.

47

F 395
5. "Drowning": on *istighrāq*, see Nicholson on *Math.* I:1111, II:305.

48

F 409
4. Rūmī quotes from a Tradition of Muhammad. For "and is truly full", CB reads "and carnelian and (*ū 'aqīq u*)".
16. Aḥmad-Muhammad. Rūmī quotes from Koran 74:35.

49

F 423
5. Badakhshan in Central Asia was famous for its rubies.
13. Cf. the story of Dhu'l-Nūn in *Math.* II:1386–1460.

50

F 436, N 14
5. "Wet-skirted": i.e. defiled and impure, of course with tears of
blood.
6. F has the misprint *jānat* for *jāmat*.
8. A play on *qaṣr* (palace) and *Qaiṣar* (Caesar).

51

F 441, N 16
Nicholson's text exhibits numerous differences.
3. "Out of your air": N tr. "From love for thee." Here CB adds an
extra couplet: "Sweet breeze blowing from Love's meadow, blow on me,
for the tidings of fragrant herbs is my desire!"
7. Oman, the southern part of the Persian Gulf, symbolizes the
Divine Ocean.
8. Koran 12:84.
10. The Lion of God was 'Alī, Muhammad's cousin and fourth
caliph. Rustam was the famous Iranian champion.
21. 'Uthmān: Sharaf al-Dīn-i Qavvāl the minstrel, see Aflākī 222,
223, 320, etc.

52

F 446
6. For the Table, see note on 6, line 16.
9. Cf. *Math.* I:2956.
11. For Ja'farī gold, see Nicholson on *Math.* I:2778 with Appendix,
IV:2060.

53

F 449, N 11
8. CB reads *jahān* (world) for *havā* (air).
9. Apposition between *murād* (object) and *murīd* (disciple).
10. For Kauthar, see note on 8 line 9.
11. I.e. "I am grieving." A play on "foot," "hand," and "head."

54

F 455, N 13
10. I.e. "If you are not a slave, but a free man of God."
14. A reference to Koran 33:53.
15. "The steely face": the mirror.

55

F 463, N 9
For the circumstances, see Aflākī 266–68; quoted by Rūmī on his deathbed, Aflākī 966–67. Nicholson's text includes F 464 (1), as does CB.
5. Muṣṭafā: Muhammad.
6. The miracle alluded to in Koran 54:1.
7. "Like the forenoon": Koran 93:1.
11. Alast: the day of God's primeval covenant with man, see Koran 7:171.

56

F 477
6. Koran 2:245.
12. Ja'far-i Ṭaiyār: heroic cousin of Muhammad, see Nicholson on *Math.* II:3565, and cf. *Math.* VI:3029–3105.

57

F 480, N 10
4. "Air": Nicholson translates "desire."
5. "The Master": N reads *uftādast* and translates "has fallen."
11. Presumably Niẓāmī the author of the epics (d. 599/1202).

58

F 484
6. See note on 26, line 3.
10. I.e. as a son of Adam, every man is heir to his ancient disobedience.

11. "Be and it is": the Divine fiat, see Koran 2:117, etc. "Ungrudging": see Koran 41:8.

13. For Korah (Qārūn) see Koran 28:76–81.

14. *Kāf* and *nūn* are the letters making up the word *kun* (Be!).

59

F 498

2. Rūmī quotes from Sanā'ī, see his *Divān* 605. Bū Ḥanīfa and Shāfi'ī were founders of schools of Islamic jurisprudence.

11. "God is sufficient": Koran 4:45.

21. See Koran 99:8.

22. Koran 99:7.

60

F 508

4. The reference is to the legend of the seven sleepers of Ephesus, see Koran 18:8–25.

61

F 524

4. Zangis: Ethiopians, black slaves—watchmen.

62

F 526

See Aflākī 237, on Fakhr al-Dīn-i Sīvāsī suddenly going mad.

1. For the idiom, see note on 12, line 3.

6. The Moaning Pillar: the palm-trunk in the Prophet's mosque at Medina which moaned when the Prophet grasped it, see Nicholson on *Math.* I:2113.

63

F 528

5. See note on 8, line 6.

64

F 532
4. Rūmī refers to the ancient romance, told by Niẓāmī in his *Khusrau u Shīrīn*. Farhād sought to dig his way through a mountain to reach Shīrīn.
6. Emending *lurkand* (gully) to *lauz-qand* (almond-sweet).

65

F 536

66

F 543
4. See Koran 23:12–14.
8. Muhammad in his Ascension disregarded the wonders of the heavens, seeking only the Presence of God. For another interpretation of the Eight Paradises, see Nicholson on *Math.* I:3498.

67

F 558

68

F 563
See Aflākī 155–56.
7. I.e. surrender reason, the great impediment to love.

69

F 566, N 21
6. "Be brave": CB reads with N *dilā zū bāsh*, "O heart, make haste."

70

F 576
5. For Ṣalāḥ al-Dīn, see note on 29, line 12.

71

F 579
3. The angel Seraphiel will blow the trumpet on the Day of Resurrection. The body once more clothes the soul in the miracle of spring.
5. Colour is a symbol for the world of phenomena, contrasted with the unicolority of the world of spirit; see Nicholson on *Math.* I:1121–35.

72

F 581
4. See Koran 59:2.
5. CB reads *zaft* (rough) for *raft* (departed). The poets liked to describe the grace of the cypress in movement.
8. "Yā Hū": the cry of the ecstatic mystic, "O He (God)!"
9. "The friend of the cave": the spirit of Muhammad.
13. A play on *chu nār* (like fire) and *chinār* (plane-tree).
19. See Koran 12:25–8.
20. For Manṣūr, see note on 16, line 4.
22. "A turnover": or, "a woman's mantle."

73

F 594
3. "Die": perhaps "space (of the distance between post-stations)," see Lane, I:1387.
9. "Why did you seek": CB reads *justam* (why did I seek).
11. This poem presumably commemorates the death of Ṣalāḥ al-Dīn Zarkūb, or perhaps his temporary absence from Rūmī's circle.

74

F 598
3. Koran 12:94.

4. Koran 12:19.
5. Koran 20:9–10.
8. See *Discourses of Rumi* 171.
9. For the famous conversion of Ibrāhīm ibn Adham (d. 160/776),
see *E.I.* II:433.
12. "Did we not open": Koran 94:1.

75

F 605
5. Cf. *Math.* IV:2403–5, on the sight as derived from the "fat" of
the eye.

76

F 614

77

F 621
8. Hārūt and Mārūt the fallen angels dwelt in a well in Babylon:
see Nicholson on *Math.* I:535.

78

F 622, N 18
5. The text of F is clearly superior to N, "to be quit of the furniture."

79

F 631
7. This poem was evidently composed to mark the end of Ramaḍān.

80

F 636

81

F 638
   3. Koran 54:1. "Good-for-nothing": reading *halanandīd* for *halapandīd*, but see F VII 461.
   4. Farhād: see note on 64, line 4. Shaddād built the paradisal Iram: see *E.I.* II 519.
   6. I.e. surrender to God's will without questioning.
   7. 'That self': God.
   10. Reading *istīzha* ('shuttle') for *istīza* ('quarrel').

82

F 644
   3. See Koran 43:38.
   7. Cf. Koran 17:22.
   11. See *Math.* IV: 3430–45 for the miracle of the Nile.

83

F 649, N 19
   6. 'Reason': Universal Reason, the first emanation of God.
   8. 'Became spirit': or, 'departed.'

84

F 656
   7. 'Surmeh': eye-salve brightening the vision.
   9. On the Day of Resurrection the faces of sinners will be black, those of the saved bright and shining, cf. Koran 75:22–4.

85

F 662

86

F 668

1. Rajab is the seventh, Sha'bān the eighth month: anciently Rajab was a month of truce.
7. 'Umar was the second, 'Uthmān the third caliph.

87

F 692
7. A play on *auḥad* (unique) and *aḥad* (one).
9. "Pegs": the great saints of every age, receiving illumination from the "Poles," see Nicholson on *Math.* II:819.

88

F 707
14. "The Friend": taking F's emendation *yār* for *pār.*

89

F 727

90

F 728
4. See Koran 15:36–8.
5. See Nicholson on *Math.* I:227.
6. Azrael is the Angel of Death. For this verse, see Aflākī 591.
7. Koran 36:27.
9. A play on *rūḥ, rīḥī, rāḥ, rāḥī.*
10. See Koran 4:157.
11. Manṣūr: Ḥallāj.

91

F 730

92

F 735
1. The proverbial elephant remembering India symbolizes the mystic recalling his divine origin.

5. Kai-Qubād was an ancient king of Persia.
6. 'The brothers of purity': the Sufis.
10. A play on *dād* (justice) and *dād* (dispensed).

93

F 745
6. A play on *ṣāf* "staining-cloth" and *ṣāf* "unsullied."

94

F 762
7. 'Uzaizī: an esteemed variety of eye-salve.
8. CB reads *maujash* (its wave) for *ābash* (its water).

95

F 765

96

F 771

97

F 779
9. For the story, see Dihkhudā, *Amthāl u ḥikam*. A Kurd who had lost his camel found it again when the moon came out, and praised the moon as though it were God.

98

F 782
11. For Jesus speaking in the cradle, see Koran 19:30–31.

99

F 791
6. CB *pastī* (low) seems better than *chustī*.
11. "This sullied cup": the physical body.

100

F 806
2. "Homeland": CB reads *ṭaraf* (side) for *waṭan*.

101

F 809
1. For the comparison of the world with a bath-stove, see *Math.*
IV:238–56.
10. Sanjar the Saljūq ruler typifies kingship.
12. For the Moaning Pillar, see note on 62, line 6.
13. "Their eyes": CB reads *nafshā-shān*.
15. "The chatter": the meaning of *dastān* is ambiguous, and the whole verse obscure.

102

F 819
7. Koran 19:25.

103

F 821
9. "The Messenger": Muhammad as intermediary and intercessor between man and God.

104

F 824
For the circumstances of composition, see Aflākī as quoted by F.
3. See Koran 53:9; i.e. "spiritual proximity."

13. Bū Saʿīd: the famous Persian mystic and poet (d. 440/1049).
14. A play on words: for Bū Yazīd, see note on 1, line 21.
16. More plays on words. Sanāʾī and ʿAṭṭār were great mystical poets.
23. Rūmī quotes Koran 50:16.

105

F 833
  1. Koran 112:1.
  8. A famous tradition states that "the believer sees by the Light of God."
  12. A play on *khar* (ass) and *khirad* (reason).
  14. "The Pole": the supreme mystic of his age, presumably Rūmī himself.

106

F 837

107

F 841
  See Aflākī 150–51.
  9. For Moses' hand, see Koran 7:105. For Khiḍar and the fish, see Koran 18:61.

108

F 853

109

F 861, N 23
  7. Koran 93:1.

110

F 863
  5. "Blind and blue" is an idiom for total blindness.

7. "Expunging": the mystical term *maḥw* is used.
11. By the sun's transforming power.
16. Cf. Koran 2:178.
18. Koran 18:18.

III

F 873

112

F 879
3. Rumi and Zangi are white and black respectively.
10. Ḥusain, son of 'Alī the fourth caliph, was slain at the battle of Kerbela by order of Yazīd.
12. For the Night of Power, see note on 43, line 5.
13. Koran 83:25.
15. Famous Sufis of old; Ma'rūf al-Karkhī died 200/816, Shiblī died 334/945.

113

F 882
4. A play on the two meanings of *sharḥ*; Rūmī has in mind Koran 94:1.
9. See Koran 100:9–10.
11. The Tablet and the Pen are Koranic terms, believed by the orthodox literally to exist in heaven.
16. Koran 27:44.

114

F 887
5. Koran 5:69.
9. Koran 50:34.
10. See Koran 79:24.

115

F 892
1. A poem in time of Ramaḍān.

2. Self-denial attaches the soul to God.
3. Rūmī quotes from Koran 100:1–2.
4. "The bow": Koran 2:63–68.
6. Koran 2:185.
10. For Jesus and the ass, see Nicholson on *Math.* II:1850.

116

F 900, N 20

117

F 909
  1. For Aflākī's account, see F *ad loc.*
  2. Koran 53:18.
  17. "Sayers of Yes": the seed of Adam, cf. Koran 7:171.
  18. "Two pieces of fat": the eyes.
  19. "A hole": the ear-hole, attracting sound as amber attracts straw.

118

F 911, N 24

119

F 919

120

F 927
  13. I.e. bad copper cannot be transmuted to gold; the doubters will never believe.

121

F 937
  10. Alast: see note on 55, line 11.
  15. Khaibar: the Jewish fortress conquered by 'Alī in A.D. 629.

16. "Five times a day": at every prayer Muhammad is proclaimed God's Messenger, and, in Shī'ite lands, 'Alī his Executor.

122

F 940

123

F 943

124

F 968
6. This and the two following lines are in Arabic.
8. Koran 34:11.

125

F 981
6. "Your own": CB reads *nau* (new) for *tū*, pairing with "old."

126

F 984
11. "Signless": spiritual.
13. See Koran 105:3, a reference to the miraculous defeat of the Abyssinian Abraha's attack on Mecca in A.D. 571.
16. Koran 8:17, the miracle of the battle of Badr in A.D. 624.

127

F 996, N 22
10. The "points" refer to the diacritical points (of certain letters) rather than to those of a compass (so Nicholson).

128

F 1001

129

F 1017
10. The five senses and the six directions.

130

F 1022

131

F 1025
4. "This sack": this physical body-prison.

132

F 1037
7. "The Veiler": God.

133

F 1047

134

F 1052
For the circumstances, see Aflākī 280–1. Rūmī was discoursing on the
tradition, "I did not see God save in a red garment."

135

F 1073

136

F 1077, N 26
3. Dhu 'l-Faqār: 'Alī's sword, symbolizing death.

7. The five senses and the four elements.
10. "The Root": God, the source of all being.

137

F 1082
6. "His tug": the mystical term *jadhba* (drawing) is used.
7. Idris is the Moslem Enoch: see Koran 19:57.
8. *Qibla:* the direction of Mecca.
15. Rūmī refers here to 1097, a shorter-lined version of this poem.

138

F 1092
7. Here as elsewhere Rūmī plays on words' double meanings.

139

F 1095
5. For Dhu 'l-Faqār, see note on 136, line 3.
9. See note on 101, verse 1.
12. Persian baths were decorated with frescoes; the symbol is of
material forms of spiritual beauty.

140

F 1103

141

F 1121
3. Rūmī quotes an Arabic rule of etiquette.
13. Nimrod died of a gnat-bite, see Nicholson on *Math.* I:1189.

142

F 1126

143

F 1131
  5. I.e. despite the unbelief of the purblind.

144

F 1136
  1. Koran 59:2.
  5. See note on 126, line 13.
  9. Rūmī refers to a tradition of Muhammad describing the Last Judgment.

145

F 1139
  3. "A hidden enemy": the carnal soul.

146

F 1142, N 27
  6. Refers to the Hegira of Muhammad. Yathrib was the ancient name of Medina.

147

F 1145, N 25
  12. Mirrors had covers of felt.

148

F 1151
  16. The dust of the beloved's feet has healing properties.

149

F 1156

150

F 1158
3. Rūmī quotes in Arabic a tradition on *memento mori*.
4. See Koran 9:40.
9. A well-known tradition, naming Muhammad as the prime purpose
of creation.

151

F 1185
5. "The mad lover": Majnūn Lailā.
6. See Koran 12:31.
11. Koran 50:16.

152

F 1195
8. The love of Sultān Mahmūd and Ayāz became proverbial: see
Math. V:2858 foll.

153

F 1201
6. The Night of Power: a night in Ramadān on which the Koran was
first revealed, when prayers are answered.

154

F 1211
4. A rare reference to the Crusaders.
5. The back of the mirror does not reflect the beauty of Joseph, sym-
bol of the Divine Beauty.
7. Cf. *Fīhi mā fīhi* 48–49.
11. "The fire": CB reads *nār-rā* for *nā-ravā*.
12. "Cursed": Koran 111:1.
13. "Brooding night": Koran 81:17. CB reads *ham-jins* (congener)
for *ham-habs* (fellow-prisoner).
14. "Docked": Koran 108:3.

155

F 1223
1. Hārūt and Mārūt: see note on 77 line 8.
3. Koran 108:1.
5. Koran 1:1 and 1:7.
6. "The houses": the 28 mansions of the moon.
7. Kai-Kā'ūs: ancient king of Persia who possessed a magic cup.
9. Koran 57:23.
10. "Testimony": invite it to become a Moslem.
12. Koran 99:1.

156

F 1235
7. I.e. "Shall I praise his physical or his moral excellence first?"

157

F 1246
7. "Hyacinthine": the curls like clusters of ears of corn.
10. Bū Lahab was an enemy of Muhammad; Bū Huraira a prominent
Companion who possessed a magic food-bag which never failed him, see
Nicholson on *Math.* V:2794.

158

F 1254
7. A play on the two meanings of *jauhar*.

159

F 1270

160

F 1288
1. Manṣūr: Ḥallāj.

161

F 1299

162

F 1301
6. The ancients believed that the emerald was a charm against snakes.
10. Koran 20:22.
12. Koran 19:25.

163

F 1304
10. "Burnt" also means "accursed."
14. The poet plays on the shapes of letters.
16. "Description" of a thing lost: perhaps "confession."

164

F 1317

165

F 1326

166

F 1335, N 28
1. Chigil in Turkestan was proverbial for its handsome inhabitants.
9. Ṣalāḥ al-Dīn Zarkūb, Shams al-Dīn's successor.

167

F 1353, N 29

3. "Return": Koran 89:27.
12. Koran 17:80 and 84:6.

168

F 1372
7. "Blood": CB reads *khvān* (table).

169
F 1380
7. For Jesus and the ass, see *Math.* II:1850.
10. CB reads *dar dardhā ai āh-gū* (You who cry ah in pain), which seems superior.

170

F 1393
9. "Impotent": i.e. "plucked clean of feathers."
18. "The seven layers": the seven heavens.
19. Joseph, after coming up from the well, waxed in beauty and power.
21. "The face": a pun on *rukh*, which also means "rook."

171

F 1397

172

F 1414
1. See Koran 20:10–12.
5. The miracle of the bird created from clay, see Koran 3:42.

173

F 1422
3. For Ja'far-i Ṭaiyār, see note on 56, line 12.
5. Adam in Moslem legend was expelled from Eden for swallowing

a grain of corn. Rūmī puns on *bū tīmār* ("heron," lit. "father of sorrow").

13. A play on *dīnār* (gold) and *dīdār* (vision).

174

F 1429

175

F 1437
9. "In peace and well-being": as of paradise, see Koran 56:88.

176

F 1447
9. "A golden calf": cf. Koran 7:146.

177

F 1458

178

F 1462, N 34

179

F 1463
4. "The tithe-collector": taking a tenth for providing safe-conduct, see Dozy II:131.
5. "Compressed *hamza*": from the hooklike shape of the orthographic sign.
8. A play on *pīrūza* (turquoise) and *pīrūz* (Victor).

180

F 1472
This poem was composed when Rūmī was sixty-two; see line 5.
9. "Blood was the food": in the womb.

11. A play on *tafsīr* (interpretation) and *taf-i sīr* ("stench of garlic," eaten by the unbelieving Jews).

181

F 1486

182

F 1489

5. Vā'il was ancestor of the Arab tribes of Bakr and Taghlib, protagonists in the famous War of Basūs; see Nicholson, *Literary History of the Arabs* 55–57.

12. A play on *nāṭiqa* ("rational soul," lit. "speaking").

183

F 1503

184

F 1508

8. For the story of Joseph and the mirror, see *Fīhi mā fīhi* 186.

185

F 1515

14. A play on *Shīrīn* and *shīrīnī* (sweetness).

186

F 1521

187

F 1531

2. I.e. the Red Sea crossing.

4. Koran 7:105.
7. See note on 141, line 13.

188

F 1538

189

F 1546
3. "Six doors": the six directions.

190

F 1554
6. Shushtar was famous for its fine robes.
10. Sanjar the great Saljuq warrior-king.
12. A play on the two meanings of *ḥalqa* (circle, knocker).

191

F 1559

192

F 1562
4. A play on *muhr* (seal) and *mihār* (toggle).
9. "Scratch a head": i.e. cajole the Beloved.

193

F 1564
9. See Koran 27:17–18.

194

F 1576

195

F 1585
 5. "In desire for": or, "in the air (*havā*) of."
 6. A play on *ṣibā* (passion) and *ṣabā* (zephyr).

196

F 1590
 3. "Meanings": spiritual realities.
 9. "From his line": i.e. decree.

197

F 1604
 1. Hātim the ancient Arab was proverbial for generosity.
 7. Koran 7:171. *Balā* = "Yes," *alast* = "Am I not (your Lord)?"
 10. The first half of this verse is in Arabic.

198

F 1610
 11. "Moon of the dormitory": the physical moon.

199

F 1615

200

F 1620